More on Evangelism in the Small Membership Church

"Royal Speidel has written this book from his personal perspectives and experiences on evangelism and church growth, and it offers valuable ideas for clergy, laity, and local churches on how to incorporate evangelism into the life of the church at various levels."

—Bishop Sudarshana Devadhar,
Greater New Jersey Annual Conference

"Weaving inspirational challenge with personal example and practical suggestion, Royal has provided an encouraging resource for leaders in churches of all sizes. In particular, *Evangelism in the Small Membership Church* is a hands-on, spiritual renewal tool to assist pastors and laity of smaller congregations to break through any self-doubts and self-imposed limitations regarding the evangelism potential of a small church. This book offers guidance by which these vital faith communities might take hold of their God-given vision with Spirit-empowered passion and discover anew the rewarding joy of proclaiming the good news of Jesus Christ to all persons."

—Rev. Greg Kroger, District Superintendent,
Glacial Lakes District, Dakotas Annual Conference

Other Books in the Series

Pastoral Care in the Small Membership Church
James L. Killen Jr.

Spiritual Leadership in the Small Membership Church
David Canada

Evangelism

in the Small Membership Church

ROYAL SPEIDEL

Abingdon Press
Nashville

EVANGELISM IN THE SMALL MEMBERSHIP CHURCH

Copyright © 2007 by Abingdon Press

This book is printed on acid-free paper.

Library of Congress Cataloging-in-Publication Data

Speidel, Royal.
   Evangelism in the small membership church / Royal Speidel.
     p. cm—(Pastoral care in the small membership church)
   ISBN-13: 978-0-687-33579-4 (pbk. : alk. paper)
   1. Small churches. 2. Evangelistic work. I. Title.

BV637.8.S64 2007
269'.2—dc22

                                  2006024179

07 08 09 10 11 12 13 14 15 16—10 9 8 7 6 5 4 3 2 1
MANUFACTURED IN THE UNITED STATES OF AMERICA

To my children
Paul and JoAnn Speidel and Sonja and
David Greiwe
And my grandchildren
Nate, Daniel, David, Charis, and Ben

Contents

Contents

Acknowledgments

I am grateful to God for the great privilege of having saving faith in Jesus Christ and for the counsel and power of the Holy Spirit. This wonderful relationship with God is the source of this book.

From the human side, my life was deeply influenced by Rita, the first love of my life for thirty-nine years. I am very grateful for the privilege of those great years of marriage.

I praise God for the second love of my life, Evelyn, who is a wise and great spiritual companion. She proofread the manuscript and gave helpful counsel in the writing.

My deep gratitude goes to editor Kathy Armistead, without whom this book would not exist. I also thank Gay Brunson, whose careful copyediting enhanced the quality of this work significantly.

My ministry for four decades was deeply shaped by God's great students of the church. Foremost among them were Lyle Schaller, George Hunter, Herb Miller, Win and Chip Arn, and most recently, Christian Schwarz.

God blessed my ministry with extremely capable laypeople, whose deep love for Jesus Christ gave life and vitality to my congregations. I learned about evangelism through those laypeople and congregations.

Embedded in various parts of the text are ideas that were shared with me by my predecessor with the General Board of Discipleship, Ralph Bauserman. I am thankful for his grace.

My prayer team was made up of the Reverends Bill Bryan, Doug Booth, Rick Carlson, the Reverend Doctors Matt Hook and Rolla Swanson, and Dr. Wendel Thompson. These men lifted me before God weekly in their prayers, and the Holy Spirit guided and strengthened me through their intercessions on my behalf. I thank God for their efforts.

Introduction

This is a book for pastors and leaders of small membership churches. If you are a small church pastor, you are likely serving two, three, or four churches. Therefore, your time is limited, as you are torn trying to meet the needs of people sometimes separated by many miles. You often spend your waking hours trying to keep your churches alive without much time to think about how to help them grow.

Because you have little time to explore resources, this book will provide you with ideas on how to improve the health of your church. As the health of your church improves, numbers may follow. In addition to presenting ideas on evangelism, this book will give ideas on how to sustain church growth, because the church provides the foundation for all evangelism. Furthermore, after coming to Christ, new Christians need the church in order to grow in Christian discipleship.

To begin a study on evangelism and church growth, invite a group in your church to spend seven weeks reading and discussing this book (two chapters a week). Discussion questions can be found at the end of each chapter, which will facilitate rich conversation that can help your church. Benefits from such reading and discussion can range from helping people with their personal walk with Jesus Christ to helping your church discover new ways God can lift the life of your congregation.

The focus of this book is twofold. First, this is a book about making disciples of Jesus Christ. Nothing is more important. Making disciples includes not only introducing people to Jesus Christ but also helping them grow in Christ. It is helping people say yes to God with their whole lives; so everything they think, say, and do is for the glory of God.

Second, it is about making disciples in the small membership church. Every small church in any setting is able to help people become disciples of Jesus Christ. Disciple making is the call of God for the small membership church in a declining rural community as well as for those in the teeming cities or growing, sprawling suburbs.

If your church has 100 or fewer in weekly worship, this book is for you. According to the General Council of Finance and Administration of the United Methodist Church, the denomination had 34,892 churches at the end of 2003. Of that number 24,795 had fewer than 100 in weekly worship attendance. Those averaging fewer than 50 at weekly worship numbered 15,770; there were 6,116 averaging fewer than 35, and 4,603 were averaging fewer than 20. Lyle Schaller says there are an estimated 200,000 churches in America with 100 or fewer in weekly worship.[1] We all like to know that we fit in life, that we belong. Obviously, small membership churches are very common, and pastors of these churches should not feel that they are outside the norm. Every pastor serving a church with less than 100 at weekly worship can know that his or her church is representative of a huge population of churches in America.

Pastors of small membership churches can find confidence in the fact that every church in the world began small. Even the large churches of today began with only a small number of people. Windsor Village United Methodist Church in Houston has weekly worship attendance of 7,700, currently the highest weekly worship attendance in the United Methodist Church in the United States. Second is the Church of the Resurrection in Kansas City with 6,500. That is followed by Mount Pisgah in Alpharetta, Georgia, with 4,950; Frazier Memorial in Montgomery, Alabama with 4,710; then Highland Park in Dallas, Texas and Glide Memorial in San Francisco, California, tied for fifth with 3,500.[2]

As God uses these big churches in a magnificent way, remember that they all had small beginnings. Those beginnings differed for each church, yet we know that each began with a few people. One or two people had a conversation about starting a new church, which then grew to 10, then to 20, and finally to 50 and more. The United Methodist Church of the Resurrection in Leawood, Kansas, has 13,000 members with a staff of 200. Adam Hamilton, the founding pastor, says they began with "four people and a dream." Virtually all large churches were small at one time.[3]

Pastors and laity of small membership churches often feel their work is insignificant compared to the work done in large membership churches. When they hear of the huge numbers of members, large gatherings of worshipers, big paid staffs, vibrant youth groups guided by paid

youth pastors, weekly offerings of tens of thousands of dollars and enormous missional giving in the large membership churches, they feel like
second-class leaders. However, God blesses the work of the small membership church and cares as much for its pastor and leaders as for the
shepherds and the ministries of a mega church.

Christian Schwarz tells of talking with a tent-making pastor in
Denmark who split his work half-time between his church and a business job. When Schwarz asked how things were going, the pastor
reflected a depressed spirit because of the small numbers in his church.
He explained that five years ago twenty people were attending worship,
and now it was only forty. Christian pointed out that this is reason to
celebrate. His church had increased worship attendance 100 percent in
five years. A mega-church averaging 20,000 would have to increase to
40,000 in five years to equal that kind of success![4]

As pastor of a small membership church you have great opportunity
to hold the chin of your congregation high. Don't just look at numbers
but look at percentages. Chances are the percentages of growth in your
church are higher than those in the big churches. God may be doing
much more in percentage growth in your church than in the largest
mega church.

Christian Schwarz argues that the small church is more effective
than the large church. In his words, "On nearly all relevant quality factors, larger churches compare disfavorably with smaller ones."[5] On what
does he base this unusual claim? First, he notes the quality of the
"minichurches" is higher than that of the mega-churches. The Institute
for Natural Church Development (NCD) has data from over 40,000
churches in 70 countries on six continents. Through an instrument
measuring the quality of a church, they discovered that 31 percent of
people attending small membership churches are involved in the
church and are using their gifts to serve Jesus Christ compared to 17 percent in the mega churches. In the small membership church 46 percent
have been integrated into a small group compared to 12 percent in the
large membership church. Also, the percentage of members attending
weekly worship is much higher in the small church than in the larger
congregations.

Statistically, small membership churches have the potential for
reaching more people than the mega churches. In its worldwide data-
base, the NCD found that churches with an average worship attendance of 51 received 32 new members over the last five years. Mega
churches averaging 2,856 received 112 during that period. The smaller

churches had 38 percent growth, while the larger ones had 4 percent growth. The mega churches were 56 times larger than the small churches. Had the mega churches received the same percentage of new people the smaller churches did, they would have received 1,792 new people in five years.

I wrote this book for churches with 100 or fewer in worship, and I hope that God will use this book to help stretch these congregations. Many of you will think it sounds more like a book for large churches, and there are a few big church references and practices that come from larger churches. However, if you are a leader in a small membership church, let your mind be stretched. Jesus Christ is able to help small membership churches offer much more than they often think they can. God is able to do big things in small churches with big thinkers.

Notes

1. Lyle Schaller, *Small Congregation Big Potential* (Nashville: Abingdon Press, 2003), 32.

2. Statistical information is from Strategic Information Services, General Council of Finance and Administration of the United Methodist Church for year-end 2003.

3. Robin Russell, "Mega Church Pastor Gives Tips for Growing Churches," *United Methodist Reporter*, February 17, 2006.

4. Christian A. Schwarz, *Color Your World with Natural Church Development* (St. Charles, Ill.: ChurchSmart Resources, 2005), 35.

5. Christian A. Schwarz, *Natural Church Development* (St. Charles, Ill.: ChurchSmart Resources, 1996), 46.

1

Evangelism: Enlarging the Fishing Club in Your Church

Peter was a professional fisherman, who Jesus said would become a fisher of people. Instead of pulling in large numbers of fish with nets, Peter would be used to reach huge numbers of people for God. His workplace would shift from a boat in the water to the dust in the street. New work tools would be needed. Nets would be replaced with words. The incentive would be reversed. His goal had been to put fish to death for food; now it would be to give the bread of life to people. The talkative Peter, who had told funny stories to pass time in the boat, would now tell eternal stories to change lives. Joining Peter would be eleven others whom Jesus enlisted into this fishing club.

Healthy, growing churches around the world constantly work at enlarging Jesus' fishing club. Jesus needs people today who are willing to change the way they are spending their time, in order to invest it in bringing people to faith in Jesus Christ. For most laity it will mean not so much leaving a job as changing what they talk about on the job and how they spend their leisure time. The larger the number of people in a church who are excited about sharing with others the new life Jesus gives people, the faster that church will grow. Enlarging the fishing club expands the kingdom of God and the church.

Evangelism: A Beautiful Word, Really

The word *evangelism* conjures up a variety of feelings. For many older Christians it has a negative connotation. They may associate it with high-pressure tactics or are afraid of being expected to evangelize. Perhaps surprisingly, for many younger churchgoers, it is a term they have never heard. Still other people, who feel neither positive nor negative, are often bewildered because they don't know what the word means.

Unfortunately, the movie *Elmer Gantry* defined evangelism in America for the last half of the twentieth century. Gantry was the flamboyant evangelist, dressed in a white suit with white shoes, who railed against evil in his tent revival meetings. Away from the glitter of the lights, he sought out women for his selfish physical pleasure. He greedily pocketed the offerings, which he lavishly spent on big cars and personal joys.

But, indeed, the word *evangelism* is a beautiful word, and the true evangelist is a wonderful person. Evangelism includes the word *angel* which means messenger. Etymologically, the "ev" comes from the Greek prefix *eu-* which means "good"; for example, "eu" in eulogy means a good word, and in euphemism, a good-sounding word. When the "eu" in Greek was put into English to make the word, *evangelism*, the *u* was made into a *v*, which is called a transliteration. So, what does evangelism mean? A good message. And an evangelist is someone who brings a good message.

Good messages and good messengers bring joy to our lives daily. A doctor reporting to family members that a surgery went very well is richly appreciated. A nurse who calls your home reporting that a biopsy shows no cancer relieves an anxious heart. Even a child bringing home a report card with straight As makes a parent glad. We love good messages and good messengers.

Evangelism, the wonderful message of God's love for us in Jesus Christ, is a joyous word. Godly persons, who lovingly tell and demonstrate this love, are glorious people. Isaiah wrote, "How beautiful upon the mountains are the feet of the messenger who announces peace, who brings good news, who announces salvation" (52:7).

Jesus was an evangelist. He "went about all the cities and villages, teaching in their synagogues, and proclaiming the good news of the kingdom" (Matt 9:35). What motivated Jesus? "When he saw the crowds, he had compassion for them, because they were harassed and helpless, like sheep without a shepherd" (Matt 9:36). Jesus saw that people without God were like ships without a rudder. They had no direction, and he cared for them.

Jesus felt that someone ought to be telling these people about God. He drew a parallel between them and a field ripe with grain. His words were, "The harvest is plentiful, but the laborers are few; therefore ask the Lord of the harvest to send out laborers into his harvest" (Matt 9:37b, 38).

Evangelist or Witness?

The church in general may have contributed to the confusion about evangelism by not clarifying its meaning. Every Christian is capable of telling the good news of Jesus Christ. Yet, just sharing a good word about God does not make one an evangelist in the New Testament sense. Evangelism as understood in the New Testament is a spiritual gift. In Ephesians 4:11, being an evangelist is listed as a gift along with being an apostle, a prophet, pastor, or teacher. Both Philip (Acts 21:8) and Timothy (2 Tim 4:5) apparently had the gift of evangelism. Matthew, Mark, Luke, and John, whose names are associated with the Gospels, were called evangelists.

Those working in the area of spiritual gifts generally believe only 10 percent of Christians are given the gift of evangelism by God. Indeed, many pastors are very effective in building and guiding congregations, but do not feel they have the gift of evangelism. False guilt is laid on people when they are expected to do the work of evangelism and they do not have the gift.

The difference between an evangelist and a witness is more like colors gradually blending into each other than like lines in the sand. All evangelists are witnesses, but not all witnesses are evangelists. By definition an evangelist is one who tells the good news of God's coming to us in Jesus Christ. Although a witness may also give verbal expression to faith, the evangelist is able to articulate the faith more easily.

People gifted as evangelists are going to meet others freely and interact fluidly. God has given evangelists the gift of relating easily with people, as evangelism is obviously so people oriented. They are very likely the "people persons" in the congregation. They may be the most effective at meeting newcomers in worship services, because they do so with greater ease.

Are there differing gifts within evangelism? Are some better at inviting? Are some better at inspiring faith through testimony? Are some better at leading others to make a definite commitment to Christ? Are yet others better at teaching people in order to evangelize them? I believe there are different gifts within the gift of evangelism as there are varieties of abilities in the gift of preaching.

Bringing people to worship is the gift of an evangelist. Some people find it very easy to invite others to join them in worship. They have the gift of winning people's confidence, so people gladly join them. Because the Holy Spirit nudges people to become disciples of Jesus Christ during worship, bringing people to worship is one purpose of evangelism.

It is said that Harry Denman, the great lay evangelist who led the Methodist Church in evangelism during the mid-twentieth century, was a master at personal evangelism. Many stories abound of his bringing large numbers of people to evangelistic services by going door-to-door inviting people. Having the ability to meet and influence people was part of God's gift of evangelism to Harry Denman. Billy Graham wrote, "Harry Denman was one of the great mentors for evangelism in my own life and ministry. . . . I never knew a man who encouraged more people in the field of evangelism than Harry Denman." [1]

Finding and Utilizing People with the Gift

How do we find people who are gifted as evangelists? Giving the congregation a spiritual gifts inventory easily does this. People express excitement when they learn what their gifts are and begin exercising them. People with the gift of evangelism need to be recognized and encouraged to use this grace.

Once the people with the gift of evangelism are identified, what can be done to utilize their gifts? Free them from other church jobs, so they can focus on evangelism. Gather these persons occasionally, so they can feed off one another. They will find encouragement together and get new ideas on how to employ their gifts. If a neighborhood outreach is done, they will inspire each other. God will help them find new ways to invite people to worship. Their gift of evangelism will also give them unique ways to inspire people in the church.

Evangelism Happens through Relationships

God captures human hearts in a variety of ways and for various reasons. However, the Holy Spirit works principally through caring relationships. We are all touched and influenced by others. Most often, faith journeys start through the relationships in the home. Timothy was moved to faith through his mother, Eunice, and his grandmother, Lois. It is a gift to have had Christian parents and a privilege to be able to influence children and grandchildren to accept Jesus Christ as Lord today.

God uses one-on-one relationships, where people share their stories. Persons of authentic faith can have an impact on friends, who have not known a relationship with God. The unchurched friends may realize that this person possesses a quality of life, a sense of purpose, and an inner peace that is lacking in their own life.

Through continued contacts where the persons of faith witness both through their Christ-like living and friendly conversations, the one without God is moved toward seeking a relationship with God. The whole evangelistic process happens as people relate to one another in restaurants, in grocery store aisles, in shops, in factories, on the internet, on cell phones, and in homes.

While serving two small-town churches in North Dakota during my first pastorate, I put on jeans during planting time and rode the tractor with farmers, visiting with them in their cabs. During harvest I rode their combines with them. I offered to pray with them after the visit before I jumped off the machine. God used those experiences to help me minister more effectively with the people.

Clergy in small churches have dead time in the afternoon, when laypeople are at work. How do you spend that time creatively for God? Meeting with people in their workplaces can be used by God. Laypeople feel honored when their clergy grace them with their presence in the places of work. Obviously, this needs to be done respectfully, making these contacts in a timely and sensitive manner. Asking for permission to stop by for a brief visit at someone's workplace helps assure acceptance of the visit.

Vulnerability Leads People to Seek God

Evangelism happens when people experience a need for something bigger than themselves. People often open up to the good news of Jesus

Christ when life has dealt them a serious blow. Ill health, financial problems, job losses, family conflicts, and failure make people feel very vulnerable. Often, simply having a child will mysteriously accentuate their sense of weakness. When we see our limitations, we become willing to accept new options and possibilities for our lives.

The wise pastor seeks out those in needy situations, first to love them and then to comfort them. Just being with people in difficult situations is very helpful to them. It also provides a wonderful opportunity to share the amazing grace of God, who is able to help us in every need. The pastoral moment becomes an evangelistic opportunity.

Evangelism happens when people come to Christ through going on a religious quest. Large numbers of unchurched Americans were raised without a religious background of any kind. Yet, every human heart has a God-shaped vacuum that is a gnawing emptiness until it is filled. People explore the possibilities for fulfillment in their lives in various ways.

Carl Jung supposedly believed that faith in God had value for emotional and psychological health. He told a patient that his life might improve if he included God in it. The patient asked how he could find God. Jung said he couldn't tell him *how* to find God, but he could tell him *where* he could find God. That place was the church.

Evangelism takes place when people see the loving grace of God in action or hear it spoken. The human heart is woefully small but wonderfully enlarged when filled with God's goodness. When people experience being with others whose lives have been filled with that divine wonder, something happens to them.

God Uses the Entire Church Experience to Win People to Christ

Evangelism certainly takes place in the church. When Jesus said he would be in the midst of two or three who were gathered together in his name, he expressed several meanings. One is that, indeed, where Christians gather in the name of Christ, there is a warm presence. Something unusual takes place. It is a gathering bigger than life.

Bringing people into the church puts them into an environment where they can meet Christ. During worship services where God's greatness is recognized, where God's power is glorified, where God's wisdom and intelligence are praised, and where God's creative genius is upheld, people experience God's love. People feeling normal human needs receive the grace of forgiveness and its cleansing power. The softening power of the Holy Spirit melts barriers in the human heart not only toward God but, often, also toward people. Being surrounded by people of faith, newcomers are inspired to become people of faith.

Millions of unchurched Americans enter congregations annually and experience God. Most often it is because they were invited, but sometimes they just wander in. God touches them first through human kindness and then through divine worship. Through worship and fellowship, God gives people that first faith, small as a grain of mustard seed.

What happens to visitors in your church? Do they get a telephone call or visit within twenty-four hours after worship? The sooner they are contacted after worship, the more effective the contact. I had a team of laity cull the attendance pads at noon on Sundays and then put the visitors' names and telephone numbers on my desk. Later that afternoon I would make my telephone calls and follow up with a letter. In urban areas many visitors come to worship wanting to remain anonymous, yet others appreciate being noticed.

There are many ways to show appreciation to visitors. Some churches have a loaf of bread with a packet of material to give visitors after the worship service. Others take bread, pies, or a mug to homes of visitors Sunday afternoon or during the week.

Evangelism Happens When Needs Are Met

Evangelism takes place when a church makes an effort to know the needs of its community. Jesus drew many followers when he healed the sick, gave sight to the blind, returned mobility to the lame, and restored the demon-possessed to their right minds and emotional health. Jesus uses the same approach to win people to himself today. Receiving loving help for practical needs turns people to the God of love.

God strengthens churches when the people of those churches care for their neighborhoods. God uses recruited and trained members of a congregation who spend time walking along the sidewalks of the community or driving within the farming area around the church in order to conduct a survey of the needs of people. By knowing and meeting the needs of the people in our church neighborhoods, we can minister to them more effectively.

When a church surveys its neighborhood, God makes several things happen. First, the residents receive a firsthand contact with someone from the church. Second, they learn that the church is a caring place with people who are genuinely interested in wanting to help. Third, the church discovers the expressed needs of people in the surrounding area. Fourth, the church can now put together ministries to meet those needs. Finally, as people feel blessed because their needs are being met, they are drawn to the church by the love of God and answer God's call to become disciples of Jesus Christ.

What types of needs can small membership churches meet? It depends on the size of the church. Every church can meet some needs. For example, assume that a community survey reveals several very needy, elderly parents living with their adult children. Even a country church with twenty-five people attending worship will have a loving soul available to sit for two hours a week with an elderly parent who can't be left alone. This would allow the adult child to go shopping or go out for an evening. A very small church can also have a drop-off program, when such persons can be brought to the church one night a week to be safely cared for.

Percept Group, Inc. makes social data available to help churches minister to people in their communities. This resource can be very useful to churches that need to learn about the people around them. As they learn more about the needs of their neighbors, churches can create new ministries that Christ will use to win people. (Percept Group, Inc. can be found on the Web at www.percept1.com/pacific/start.asp.)

Here is a big church example that illustrates creativity, giving it small church application. Pastor Jack Stephenson of Anona United Methodist Church in Largo, Florida, tells of a dramatic evangelistic ministry through the use of Percept. The church had a morning preschool with an enrollment of fifty. Wanting to know their community needs better, they discovered through Percept that 73 percent of the community was made up of either single, working parents or married couples with both parents working outside the home. So they expanded their preschool to all day and added before- and after-school programs. Today they have 316 children with a waiting list of 98. Many of their new members come from these parents, because the church is ministering to their children. Jesus Christ wins people to himself and his church today as the church meets their needs.

This kind of ministry can be done on a smaller scale in small membership churches. If small membership churches look at data about their communities, they will find needs to which they can minister. It is all about love. Are we open to loving? Are we open to losing ourselves for the cause of Jesus Christ? Jesus wins people to himself through this kind of service.

Evangelism's Bottom Line

The goal of evangelism is to help people enter into a personal relationship with Jesus Christ. Everything in evangelism has the goal of making disciples of Jesus Christ. The good news of God's coming to us in Jesus Christ is to redeem people. God is in the renewing business, providing new life to all. Through Jesus' death on the cross, God offers people freedom from guilt. Troublesome thoughts of past sins can be overcome. Peace of heart can replace pained feelings of failure and sin.

The good news of Jesus Christ is that God has come to reconcile people to God. It is to connect people with God, so they can communicate with God through prayer. People reconciled with God begin reading the Bible, allowing God to speak to them through the recorded word.

When people are truly touched by the good news of God's love, they come to realize that all of life is about loving. We are saved from our limited selves to a much bigger life with God. The Holy Spirit helps us change from self-centeredness to an other-directed life. Instead of focusing just on our own needs, we want to lift the lives of others. God created us for good works; after entering into a relationship with God, we receive grace to invest our lives in others. That includes not only giving of self and energy, but also the giving of financial resources.

God wants sons and daughters who are in love with God. Jesus Christ wants followers who spend their lives loving God, themselves, and those around them. The Holy Spirit wants hearts that are open to divine direction. God wants minds that are open to loving thoughts and are shut off to self-centered ideas.

Winning new people to Christ and the church is easier than reactivating the inactive. It is very difficult to convince inactive members to return to the church unless they become reconciled with their reason for leaving. Yes, sending them the newsletter for a few years is good to do. But we all have so little time, and spending it on reaching new people generally yields more favorable results. Obviously, the inactive are important to God, but for some reason God is able to touch new people for Christ and the church far more easily than those who have turned away from the church.

Discussion questions

1. What happens to visitors in our church?
2. Who are the "people persons" in our church?
3. How and when will we discover persons with the gift of evangelism in our church?
4. What structure can we put together to help them use this gift in our church?
5. What will we do to learn the needs of the community around our church?
6. Who will follow through to create ministries to meet those needs and when?

Resources

1. A spiritual gifts inventory helps identify people in a congregation with the gift of evangelism. There are many such inventories available. C. Peter Wagner was a pioneer in this work. Two of his books on this topic are: *Finding Your Spiritual Gifts* and *Your Spiritual Gifts Can Help Your Church Grow.*
2. Surveys to discover the needs of your community can be purchased. Or you can create your own survey. It is critical that an in-house survey have both the right questions and the right wording of the questions. If you put together your own survey, share it with several pastors and knowledgeable laity to get it right before you use it. Even ten questions could give a small membership church some good information about its neighborhood.
3. Many denominational headquarters use Percept so a local church can get data free of charge. Their website is: www.percept1.com/pacific/start.asp.

Note

1. Billy Graham, Foreword to *Prophetic Evangelist: The Living Legacy of Harry Denman* (Nashville: Upper Room Discipleship Resources, 1993).

2

Vision: Having "God Eyes" for Big Possibilities in Your Church

Every small membership church is uniquely positioned, so it has its own possibilities. Small membership churches are like individuals before God. As God has a will for persons, so God has a will for churches. We serve a God of reality, who knows our circumstances better than we know them and takes into consideration all aspects of our lives.

For example, it is not very likely God's will that a man or woman who is five feet tall become a professional basketball player, or that a man weighing 125 pounds become a professional football player. Likewise, it is not likely God's will that a small, rural church in a declining area become a mega church. However, short athletes can excel and become very successful in several sports, and small membership churches can succeed in becoming excellent churches. God takes into consideration the situation of the small church. God's will is that small membership churches, in communities everywhere, live up to their potential. As it is God's will that every human being reach his or her greatest potential, so it is God's will that every small membership church do the same.

The number of persons surrounding small membership churches has an obvious impact on church outreach. Having God Eyes for big possibilities in a rural church with few people surrounding it means that it must insist on being a church of highest quality and intentional in seeking to reach every person in the community or area. Small rural churches serving God with high quality worship and meaningful programs can reach persons previously uninterested. Furthermore, serving Jesus Christ with higher excellence will give the small rural church motivation to reach out to the unchurched, who may have been previously ignored. And there are *always* those the church has ignored.

Exurbia is made up of communities outside the suburban area. God's will for the small membership church in exurbia, where newcomers are arriving from the city, might be very different from God's will for small churches in suburbs or cities. God sees new possibilities for small membership churches in expanding exurbia, where new growth is surging.

When large neighborhoods surround small membership churches in suburbs and cities, there is obviously much potential for church growth. Often heterogeneous populations surround small membership churches in these settings. What is God's will for the small membership church in the city made up of a variety of ethnic cultures? Can God see such a church becoming a small United Nations?

Vision Is Seeing Possibilities

Life is always filled with possibilities. President Ronald Reagan enjoyed telling the story of twin boys. One of them was taken into a room filled with new toys, and the lad began to cry. He was overwhelmed and became afraid that he might break them in his playing. The other was taken into a room filled with manure, and he became excited. He began digging saying, "There has to be a pony in there somewhere." The small membership church will reach its highest potential only with visionary leaders. The pastor and lay leaders need to be optimistic, believing that God has wonderful possibilities for their church. Small church pastors and laypersons can be very proud of their churches, if they have a great vision for their churches and are doing everything possible to let Jesus Christ fulfill that vision.

Smallness does not equate with mediocrity. Excellence can permeate small membership churches. Their facilities can be very well structured and beautifully decorated. Small membership churches can have very fine programs and exciting worship services. They can be managed more effectively than large membership churches.

Eleanor Roosevelt said, "No one can make you feel inferior without your consent." The small congregation does not need to feel it is a second-class church because it does not have the numbers of the large church. By focusing on Jesus Christ and seeking to serve him, a small membership church can allow the Holy Spirit to fill it with new vision and enthusiasm. It can be filled with confidence, and joy can permeate the church while it helps develop disciples of Jesus Christ. It all depends upon whether a church has God Eyes for big possibilities. Big possibilities have more to do with quality than with quantity. If a church is to experience growth in numbers, it will happen only after the church develops excellence in its work.

Ezekiel lived with his fellow exiles in a strange land. Filled with gloom, they wandered around hopeless, feeling like dead skeletons. In the following passage, Ezekiel recounts how God showed him the remedy for bone rattling despair:

> He said to me, "Mortal, can these bones live?" I answered, "O Lord GOD, you know." Then [GOD] said to me, "Prophesy to these bones, and say to them: O dry bones, hear the word of the LORD. Thus says the Lord GOD to these bones: I will cause breath to enter you, and you shall live. I will lay sinews on you, and will cause flesh to come upon you, and cover you with skin, and put breath in you, and you shall live; and you shall know that I am the LORD." (Ezek 37:3-6)

God gave Ezekiel a vision of new possibilities. No matter what your church is like, do you believe that God can make dry bones come to life again?

Believing God can bring new life to your church takes deep and abiding hope, which ought to be related to your call. It takes faith to believe that Jesus Christ can bring new life to individuals. Do you believe that every person needs Jesus Christ? Your answer to that question will have a huge impact on your ministry and on your church.

Turning Vision into a Mission Statement

A vision begins with God. What does Jesus Christ want for your church? Ask the people to pray for God's help in determining the vision for your church. What are the fundamental goals of your church? What can you accomplish when you work cooperatively with God?

As the church determines a vision for the future, it is not enough to talk about it. The vision needs to be put on paper, in order to clarify it and make it more concrete. What is the mission of the church? Why does it exist? What are its goals? What is it trying to accomplish for Jesus Christ?

Here are other questions your church can raise as you consider what to include in a mission statement: To whom are you wishing to minister? Who is your target audience? Small membership churches, whether in the country or in a small town, will want to focus on people in their neighborhoods. Small membership churches in the city or suburbs also need to focus on the surrounding communities; however, because their communities may be so diverse, these churches may wish to center on a particular group within the neighborhood. For example, they may wish to reach younger families by creating programs to meet their specific needs.

A lofty vision put into a specific, concrete mission statement that is taken seriously will create an energized church. A general vision with a feel-good, fuzzy mission statement will create a bland church. Many congregations focus on being welcoming and loving communities of faith. Every church needs a warm and accepting atmosphere; however, a church-changing mission statement needs more than kindness and love. The church's mission statement needs to include disciple making.

God is in the redeeming and renewing business. Jesus Christ died in order to change lives. It is both God's will and the desire of people for a church to be in the life-changing business. Erwin McManus wrote, "People are looking for something worth believing in, somewhere to belong, and something to become."[1] Healthy people want to continue to grow. Married couples want help in their relationships. Parents need support and guidance for their children. Communities need help in supporting the needy. Indeed, God needs the small church to help minister to the nation and save the world.

What kind of mission statement can you write that will help your church be a place where men, women, boys, and girls experience spiritual transformation? What kind of mission statement will help your congregation become a church where people, indeed, find new life? What does God use in the weekly church experience to deepen faith and sanctify people? If evangelism, worship, education, service, and fellowship are fundamental, how can the core of each of these areas of church life be incorporated into a mission statement?

With a Vision on Paper, Then What?

A pastor told me that his congregation contracted a church consulting firm to develop a package of renewal plans for their church. No doubt the congregation paid big dollars for this service. The consultants put together a package of suggested steps for revitalization. However, many months later the recommendations from the firm were sitting on a shelf in the pastor's study collecting dust.

Mission statements can also collect dust, or they can be used to let the Holy Spirit guide a church in becoming a true agent of change. How can that happen? First, the mission statement needs to be kept before the congregation constantly, either through worship, the worship bulletins, or newsletters. Periodically reading the mission statement together in church council meetings also helps.

But there is more. How can the church know if it is living up to its vision? Can an evaluation form be written that would help the church know if it is, indeed, following its mission statement? Can measurements be determined for the various aspects of the mission statement? For example, if a church has a stated goal of making disciples of Jesus Christ, how can it determine if that is happening? Putting numbers to the evaluation helps the church measure its success. A wise businessperson said, "If you can't measure it, you can't manage it." A wise church manages its mission statement with numerical measurements in order to learn if it is fulfilling its vision.

Visioning the Unchurched as Possible Kingdom People

Jesus wants every church to first reach the people in its neighborhood. Luke reports in the book of Acts that Jesus told his disciples, "You will be my witnesses in Jerusalem, in all Judea and Samaria, and to the ends of the earth" (1:8). The disciples' first responsibility was to witness locally. Jerusalem was their neighborhood. The same principle for evangelizing exists today. We need to first reach the people in our communities.

Every community has unchurched people or inactive church members in it. Gallup pollsters have been reporting for decades that 40 percent of Americans are in worship once a week. Other students of the church put the figure at 32 percent. This means that 60 percent to

68 percent of Americans are not in worship each week. Some church scholars believe that 60 percent of Americans are affiliated with a church, but that still leaves 40 percent unchurched.

These people live in your community. Some may have more material possessions than they could ever use, but these people are lost. Others are struggling daily to make ends meet, and they do not know the strength that the Holy Spirit can infuse in believers. They are part of the group Jesus was ministering to as recorded by Matthew, "When he saw the crowds, he had compassion for them, because they were harassed and helpless, like sheep without a shepherd" (9:36). Whether wealthy, middle class, or poor, all people are in need of the redeeming work of Jesus Christ. God wants these men, women, youth, and children to be God's children. God created us and not only wants to enjoy us but also wants us to have the joy of walking with God.

Paul, in writing to his younger colleague Timothy, refers to "God our Savior, who desires everyone to be saved and to come to the knowledge of the truth" (1 Tim 2:3-4). The Gospel of John says, "For God so loved the world that he gave his only Son, so that everyone who believes in him may not perish but may have eternal life" (John 3:16). This means that God loves neighborhoods and communities, and that Jesus Christ willingly died for our neighbors. God is pursuing all persons for a love relationship, and God needs the small membership church to help its neighbors find that relationship through Jesus Christ.

Time blinds us to new possibilities for people around us. Every community has unchurched people. They may have been the subject of gossip, often causing the church not to be interested in loving them. No matter, if people have been considered outcasts because of behavior unacceptable to the community, God sees possibilities of new life for them. Can the church have God Eyes to envision these people as kingdom people? I heard a bishop say that he wept when 200 of the 700 churches in his conference did not bring even one person to Christ and the church during that year. How can God give these churches a vision to reach the world for Jesus Christ?

Visualizing a Transformational Church

Only a transformational church has a future. People are too busy to get involved with feel-good churches, where life changes are not encouraged or expected. The unchurched, and the inactive as well as the active members are looking for God to help them live better lives. Churches offering this help will win the hearts of the people.

Small membership churches can become transformational churches. It begins with the vision of the church. According to the Gospel of Matthew, Jesus' last instructions to his disciples were that they should make disciples of all people. Churches that take this commission seriously are usually growing churches.

Visionary churches are transformational churches. When churches make disciples, people are transformed, and only transformational churches grow. They make it their business to help people find a profound faith in God that changes them. Jesus once met a woman at Jacob's well, and she was changed. She excitedly went into her village and brought others to the well to meet Jesus. This ageless contagion of people changed by Jesus bringing others to find the new life is prevalent today. This is how God enables churches to evangelize.

Churches with a vision want nothing more than to do God's will. Jesus directs their goals. Everything they do is centered on helping people find saving faith in Jesus Christ. It is important to not only desire to follow God's will for your church, but also to believe that God will help you fulfill your mission statement. God spoke through Isaiah in chapter 43, verse 19, "I am about to do a new thing; . . . do you not perceive it?" God wants to bring about new life in your church, while you may think your church is hopelessly stuck. Remember what the angel said to Mary, "For nothing will be impossible with God" (Luke 1:37).

An Inspiring Story of Vision from the Past

George Hunter tells the following story in his book *To Spread the Power.*

> One morning in 1881, the Reverend C. C. McCabe sat on a train heading toward the Pacific northwest of the United States. In a few days he would be leading the planning, later the fundraising, for planting Methodist churches over much of Oregon, Idaho, and Washington. Years before, he had been an influential chaplain in the Civil War. Now he was leader of new church extension for the Methodist Episcopal Church. . . . The Methodist Church was starting

more than one new congregation a day. Some months they averaged two new churches a day.

An article in McCabe's morning newspaper featured a speech delivered in Chicago by Robert G. Ingersol, the famous agnostic philosopher, to a convention of the Freethinkers Association of America. Ingersol's speech declared that "the churches are dying out all over the earth; they are struck with death." When the train stopped at the next town, McCabe sent a telegram to Ingersol, still at the convention:

Dear Robert:

"All hail the power of Jesus' name"—we are building one Methodist Church for every day in the year, and propose to make it two a day!

C. C. McCabe

Word about the telegram was leaked, and someone wrote a folk hymn that was sung throughout the Pacific Northwest in preaching missions and camp meetings, brush arbors and Sunday evening services. The song dramatized the frontier Methodist people's quiet confidence in the power of what they offered people:

> The infidels a motley band,
>   in counsel met, and said:
> "The churches are dying across the land,
>   and soon they'll all be dead."
> When suddenly, a message came
>   and caught them with dismay:
> "All hail the power of Jesus' name,
>   We're building two a day."
>
> "We're building two a day, Dear Bob,
>   We're building two a day!
> All hail the power of Jesus' name,
>   We're building two a day." [2]

Vision Begins with the Leadership

The whole spiritual tone of a church is set by its leaders. Leaders of the church have to set the stage. Pastors and leaders of the church who watch pornography on television or the computer cannot help their men, women, and youth know how to have clean minds. Pastors and church leaders who are not pray-ers can hardly help their people develop deep prayer lives. Your youth and children need adult models in their church whom they can follow. You can't take people to where you haven't been. You need to be spiritual leaders in your church.

The closer you walk with God the more wonderful your life will become, and through that close walk you will be used by God to help others find the abundant life in Christ, which brings purpose, power, and a peace that passes all understanding.

Discussion questions

1. Do we believe that every person needs Jesus Christ?
2. If we have a mission statement, how can we improve it to more effectively make disciples of Jesus Christ? If we do not have a mission statement, how will we begin the process to create one?
3. Do we publicize the mission statement, so that all our people know it?
4. What programs can we create to help fulfill our mission statement?
5. What instrument of evaluation do we use in order to learn the degree we are fulfilling our mission statement?
6. Does it contain specific numbers to make our measurement most meaningful?
7. Who are the unchurched in our community, and how can we reach them for Jesus Christ?

Notes

1. Erwin Raphael McManus, *The Unstoppable Force* (Orange, Calif.: Yates & Yates, 2001), 97.
2. George G. Hunter, III, *To Spread the Power: Church Growth in the Wesleyan Spirit* (Nashville: Abingdon, 1987), 19-20.

3

Worship: Creating Exciting Worship Services That Win People for Christ

Much evangelism happens through corporate worship. The Holy Spirit most effectively woos people to faith in Jesus Christ through energizing and meaningful worship services. Countless people come to saving faith in Jesus Christ through worshiping with a congregation.

Worship: God's Biggest Magnet

Evangelism takes place within churches, and worship is the biggest magnet God has to draw people to your church. It is central to the life of every church, so whatever happens during your worship time will determine what kind of church you have. Worship is the heart of the church. It is the strongest factor that will draw people to your church. Everything in your church feeds off the worship service. The quality of your worship service will determine what kind of Sunday school program you have. The number of kids you have in youth group, as well as the amount of money you have available for missions, will be determined by your worship service.

Churches that are growing and effectively reaching people for Jesus Christ offer quality worship with excellent preaching. Through exciting worship people are lifted in spirit; their minds are informed; their faith is strengthened; they are given models of spirituality; they leave the service feeling that the Spirit of Christ has been imparted to them. They feel challenged to live more godly lives. Often they have a bounce in their step, because they have been offered healing and hope. The refreshing, spoken word of God has intersected with them at some of the most painful points of their lives.

Therefore, the most important thing for every church is to provide the best kind of worship experience people can have, and the worship experience begins in the parking lot! Is everything well marked? Are there signs telling people how to get in and how to get out? Do you have one or two places, close to the church, reserved for visitors and persons with handicaps, giving them the closest access to the church? If you have snowy winters, is your parking lot snowplowed before worship? Are your walks salted?

Leaders Set the Example

If you are a layperson, I trust you are in worship every weekend except when you are sick or out of town. Worshiping God is fundamental to the Christian life. I used to tell my congregation during worship, "I am here, not because I am being paid, but because I am a Christian. Worship is part of my Christian life." On my last Sunday before retiring, I told my congregation, "In my retirement, if you ever hear that I was not in worship on the weekend, I want you to call me a hypocrite or a phony." If we love God with all our heart, mind, soul, and strength, we will worship God weekly. How can we guide our churches to make disciples for Christ if we ourselves are not completely dedicated to him?

Many years ago a retired pastor came to worship in my congregation. I invited him into my office between the Sunday services for a cup of coffee and some private conversation. A lay liturgist came into my office, where the liturgists met prior to worship. In her presence, the clergyman extolled the virtues of retirement. Then he said, "Retirement is great. If I don't feel like going to church, I sleep in." I was embarrassed before this layperson. What kind of example did this clergy set? How could he lead his congregation in their growth in faith in Jesus Christ when he didn't think worship was important?

Preaching or Teaching: Still the Bottom Line

Preaching or teaching during worship is considered by laity the single most important part of the service. People hunger for excellent preaching or teaching. Music is wonderful and utterly important in worship, and all of us should do our best to provide our people with the very best music. Some people will come to worship because they love the music. However, the vast majority of people come to worship to hear the word of God proclaimed. Virtually every survey shows laity want excellent preaching in worship more than anything else.

I believe it is important to see preaching also as teaching. Many churches use the word *teaching*, instead of *sermon*, in the worship bulletin. Younger adults may be more attracted to teaching than preaching. The expression "Don't preach at me" used to be common. However, the words "Don't try to teach me" are virtually never heard. Teaching has a more pleasant ring, and thus may be a more acceptable word to younger adults. Jesus was most often called *rabbi*, which means master. However, it was used by Jews to refer to their teachers. The Gospels refer to much of Jesus' work as teaching. Even in the Great Commission, we are told to teach everything he commanded us.

Preaching is a great privilege and a unique opportunity. Only as the congregation gathers for worship does the pastor have opportunity to communicate with the entire flock. God gives pastors a terrific gift of being able to touch people deeply as they come to drink in and soak up the word of God as it comes from their pastor.

People are seeking religious experiences. Augustine's observation sixteen hundred years ago is still fresh today: "Lord, our hearts are restless until they find their rest in thee." When John Wesley experienced Christ profoundly on Aldersgate Street at the age of thirty-six, his life was changed. Only transformational churches are growing. People want a church where their lives are changed by God. They want to know about this book called the Bible. They want a faith that helps them make sense out of life. God wants to give people rock-solid values on which they can build their lives. Good preaching and teaching will do that. It will help people develop deeper commitments that bring great strength.

Preaching Style

Traditions and way of life dictate the most effective style of preaching or teaching. Some people expect a lot of emotion in the pulpit, while others prefer less. Preaching with fire does not need to mean preaching with less light.

Presentation style has to be consistent with who you are. You have to present your sermons in the most natural way. The conversational style is popular, and the Holy Spirit uses that beautifully. Others prefer a more dramatic style, and God uses that also. It is said that Jonathan Edwards stood motionless, reading from a manuscript. I have not seen many preachers able to do that today with much effectiveness.

No matter what our setting, it is essential that we stay true to ourselves. We can learn by watching others preach, but mimicking someone else likely will not be very effective.

Do you preach from a manuscript or from an outline? Again, everyone is unique. Preachers use a manuscript effectively when it becomes a guide to refer to, not a master holding them to every word. Writing a manuscript gives God the opportunity to help a preacher think through ideas and shape them into compelling words. Manuscripts can help the preacher express thoughts clearly and preach or teach without fumbling around for words.

When Do You Have Your Sermon Ready?

Preparing for preaching is different for all of us. We approach preparation differently, because we are different. We are different in what we know, what we understand, how we approach life, and how we preach. No one homiletical style fits all.

Whether you work from an outline or a manuscript, you have to spend time in preparation. It makes no difference whether your preaching is textual, expositional, or topical; you have to put in prep time. The thoughtful people in your church can tell whether or not you have done your homework. The Holy Spirit is given more opportunity to move powerfully upon people's hearts when their pastor has prayed, studied, and worked on his or her sermons.

The problem with preparing sermons is the same as the problem with time management. Nobody is standing at your side telling you to work at it. Everything is completely up to your choosing; and unfortunately, it is very easy to put off working on the sermon until Thursday, Friday, or even Saturday. I confess to having gone through various phases of sermonic preparation. During most of my early and middle years, I worked one week at a time, sometimes even on Saturday afternoon, preparing the sermon for the following Sunday morning. However, I became deeply influenced by the example set by Frank Harrington, senior pastor of Peachtree Presbyterian Church (USA) in Atlanta. At that time this congregation had the largest worship attendance in the denomination, and Dr. Harrington was in the habit of preparing his sermons at least three months in advance. So I began writing my sermons at least one to two months in advance. God used that kind of preparation in a number of ways. First, my messages were so much better thought out. Second, it gave the Holy Spirit opportunity to massage the messages in my heart and mind. They were not only on paper but were also in my heart. Third, I was able to give my scriptures, texts, and sermon titles to my music people a month in advance. The choir was able to choose music that fit my sermon. I was always able to give my secretary the bulletin material for the sermon one or two weeks in advance.

When do you have your sermons ready for the next Sunday morning? Would you consider working to prepare them a month or two in advance? If not a month or two, how about a week or two?

You will most likely have your sermons ready early and consistently if you give your sermonic work first priority in your weekly schedule. Years ago a popular model for weekly scheduling was to spend the morning in the study working on sermons, the afternoon completing administrative tasks, and the evening participating in meetings or visitation.

God can still use that model to create effective preachers. Wise pastors create a schedule that allows God to have the finest messages prepared through them, and then stick to it religiously. Nothing will be more important for reaching people for Jesus Christ than an excellent weekly sermon.

Lectionaries and Other Resources

Do you use the lectionary to guide your homiletical schedule? Using a lectionary can have at least three advantages. The lectionary can give a pastor consistent direction, so he or she always knows where to move in preparation. Second, the lectionary can keep the pastor in the scriptures, so the sermons are biblically based. Third, the lectionary can be effective in preventing a pastor from riding a hobbyhorse in the pulpit or constantly repeating a subject, which is a temptation when preaching topically.

Most ministers are willing to share and use one another's ideas and sermon illustrations, but we don't want to plagiarize material. Giving credit where credit is due by acknowledging the author and the original source keeps you honest and honors God.

Harry Emerson Fosdick, the great author and preacher at Riverside Church in New York City, was vacationing in the country one summer. He attended a small church in the community. As he listened to the sermon, he realized it was one he had written. The young pastor was using it word for word. Upon greeting the lad at the door, Fosdick said, "I wrote that sermon you just preached." With a brightened face, the young pastor responded, "You did? Well, you keep writing 'em, and I'll keep preaching 'em." Had the young man acknowledged what he was doing, the sermon would have been just as effective, and he would have been a more honest person.

The Small Membership Church Can Be High Tech

We have a high-tech God who can help you use technology to enhance your sermons. If you can get a screen or use a white wall in your church to project your sermon outline, God will bless your sermons more than you know. We live in a visual society. People watch an average of five hours of television daily, and when they aren't sitting in front of the TV, they may be peering at a computer monitor. Sermons that are enhanced with outlines and other visuals projected on a screen are much more meaningful to most people. When people can see what they are hearing, it makes a deeper impression on them. Visual learners get more from the message.

If space permits, small churches can have a front screen for the congregation and another screen high in the back of the sanctuary so the pastor and choir can see the same images that the congregation is seeing. Pastors can preach from the outline they see on the back screen. Obviously, projecting the outline and images has to be very well coordinated to be effective. You have to have a highly capable and responsible person running the projector for you. Otherwise, if you are relying on the screen for your outline, you are in trouble if the person at the projector puts up the wrong images.

It may be a stretch for most small churches, but one way to enliven your announcements is by videotaping them during the week. One church makes this type of video and features a man and woman in their thirties, who have bright smiles and abundant energy. The videotape is played at the beginning of the service, and the announcements are truly interesting and exciting. This is an excellent way to present announcements, which often become too drab and too long.

Additional ideas for making the worship service more meaningful include using the screen to show the call to worship, the scripture, and the words of the anthem. Small membership churches can have good sound systems and well-trained people running them. If your preaching can't be heard, it is meaningless. Pastors of quality small membership churches see that a sound check is completed before each service begins. God is able to make worship most meaningful when everything can be easily heard and understood.

I used to have my sermons printed so people could pick up a copy before they went into the sanctuary to worship. If you tape your sermons so copies are available after worship, that will be another enhancement. People spend many hours driving, and they will listen to your sermon again during the week.

Preaching or teaching is the pastor's number one responsibility each week. The life of the church depends on what the people hear from you. Pray about the sermons. Ask God to help you with your preparation and presentation. Preaching out of your own life experiences touches lives deeply for Jesus Christ.

Funding High-Tech Equipment

Small membership churches may feel they do not have resources to obtain screens, projectors, and computers necessary for high-tech worship enhancement. However, there are financially endowed people in virtually every congregation who would donate money for such equipment if they catch the vision and spirit of this avenue for evangelism. When people understand that such equipment can help reach more people for Jesus Christ, they understand the magnitude of such gifts. Older people who are able to give are often concerned about bringing younger people into the congregation. One way for them to help attract younger people is to contribute to high-tech equipment needed to produce the visual enhancements that draw more young people to worship and hold their interest.

Developing Music That Tunes Up People's Lives

Small membership churches can have excellent music during worship. Most churches have vocalists who can bring joy to the heart. Also, churches can augment their vocal music by using talented people in the community. Schools may have madrigal singers, with a repertoire that includes Christian music, who would feel honored to be invited to help a congregation worship God.

The wise pastor of a small membership church works at incorporating music into at least 40 percent of the worship service. In both the Jewish temple and the Christian church, God has used delightful music to bring hope, joy, and grace. Music can touch the soul in places words cannot reach.

The organ has been used for hundreds of years to inspire hearts. While the organ is still the primary instrument in most churches, musicians playing compositions written for piano and organ together create a sound joyous to many. These two instruments can add a new dynamic to a service.

Instruments frequently used in secular music (guitars, drums, and synthesizers) have been widely used in American churches for twenty to twenty-five years. The reason is that people feel more comfortable worshiping Jesus Christ on Sunday with music they hear in their cars as they drive down the road Monday through Saturday. The guitar is the most popular instrument in America, and people enjoy hearing that sound in worship. Virtually every church has young people who play the guitar and consider being asked to play in church an honor. God is wonderfully able to touch hearts through uplifting, stirring music. Having at least two pieces of special music in addition to three hymns adds zest to worship. That special music could be a choir, an ensemble, or a solo. Great singing makes preaching easier and more effective. God also uses liturgical dance as well as signing a song.

Inspiring music videos are widely available today for churches with limited musical talent. Smiling faces and joyous hearts will occupy the pews as the congregation listens to the grand orchestral strains of "How

Great Thou Art" and watches the screen for the accompanying scenes of mountain grandeur. An effective pastor can put together an entire service, week after week, using video music.

Giving an Invitation to Accept Christ through Communion

The sacrament of Holy Communion is a means of grace by which our faith is deepened. Jesus instituted this sacrament to give us a way in which we can remain spiritually connected with him. However, Jesus Christ can also use Holy Communion for evangelism. People can come to put their faith in the Savior through experiencing the sacrament.

The pastor can instruct the congregation to receive the elements with their arms outstretched and palms open. They can be instructed to invite Christ into their lives as they receive the bread and cup. In accepting these physical symbols of Christ, they accept Christ himself.

Up-tempo Worship Enhances Church Growth

When we were in my study preparing to begin the worship service, I used to tell our liturgists, "People come to worship and not to watch us walk." Walking to the pulpit or getting a choir in place can be done during a hymn. After the hymn is finished, there is no need to have dead spots in the service. The person leading the next segment of the service can be in place, ready to begin. Smooth transition from one segment of the service to the next enhances the worship experience.

God uses services that flow from one part into the next. This kind of smooth transition is what people experience on television. Therefore, this is the kind of movement they find more interesting in their local churches. Long, silent delays, except for silent prayer, make people feel uneasy and cause the service to be boring.

Worship Begins in Your Parking Lot

The worship experience begins in the parking lot. Small membership churches can have parking lot ushers, who serve as outdoor greeters.

Then, once people enter your building, what happens next? First impressions are very important. When people walk into your church, what will they see? Will it be nicely decorated walls or paint peeling? Will they see clean floors and nice carpeting? Is everything neat, or will they see clutter? It will be worth paying somebody from your community $25.00 to walk through the building and point out what they see. People who walk by a burned-out light bulb three times will get used to it and not notice it anymore. People who attend regularly become blinded to their church's building faults, whereas fresh eyes will immediately spot them. Keeping the church grounds and buildings in good shape, honoring God, will help improve worship attendance.

If visitors have children, are your signs helpful, giving clear directions to the nursery and other Sunday school rooms? If children are expected to sit through the service, do you have some crayons and religious pictures and puzzles they can color?

Will there be greeters at your front door to help visitors with questions? Will your greeters have the answers, or will they be able to quickly direct the people to someone who does have answers?

Is your nursery freshly painted and always immaculately clean, so that children can play safely, even on the floor? Are the toys washed and sanitized? Will new people be happy leaving their children in your nursery? Is it well staffed, so there is always a proper adult/child ratio? Visitors and members alike will want the very best facility and appropriate care for their children.

Children's Sermons beyond the First Two Pews

How can the entire congregation enjoy and appreciate the children's sermon? Having the children visible to the people, so each child can be seen by the entire church, makes the experience much more meaningful. Often the children are asked to sit and are hidden to anyone beyond the first two pews. If they can't be seen, even on the top platform of the chancel, have them stand.

Also, the congregation must hear the conversation between the leader and the children. The leader of the children's sermon should have a microphone, and then he or she can also repeat for the congregation what the children say during dialogue. A well thought-out message with the children fully visible and the conversation fully heard can be enjoyable and instructive to the children and interesting to the adults watching and listening in the pews.

Taking a Visitor-Friendly Offering

How about your offering? When we took the offering, we said, "If you are a visitor here today, sit back and relax as the members of our church give their tithes and offerings to the work of Jesus Christ." Some churches do not even take an offering. You have to find the offering boxes in the narthex if you want to give. Do everything you can to make visitors feel comfortable, so God can touch their hearts in your church.

Discussion questions

1. How can we make our parking lot and worship more visitor friendly?
2. What can we do to let God use our building more effectively for worship?
3. What changes in our worship services will bring more people?
4. Pastor, when do you have your sermons ready, and how do you feel about that?
5. Pastor, how can you get feedback from the congregation to let God use your sermons most effectively?
6. What would it take to get projector or computer technology into our church to enhance our worship experience?
7. If we already have technology in our worship services, how can we improve it?

4

Relationships: Helping God Raise the Love Factor in Your Church

People are wooed to Jesus Christ by the power of love, and God uses loving relationships in a church to make that happen. Evangelism, the sharing of the good news of salvation in Christ, is most effective when bathed in the atmosphere of a loving congregation. God came to us in Jesus Christ, because of God's loving heart, and God uses loving people to help others accept that wonderful love.

Life Is All about Love

God created the church out of love, and God wants the church to spread that love throughout the world. God created the world in order to have children to love. When those children disobeyed and went astray, God lovingly came to earth through Jesus Christ in order to restore that relationship. The Holy Spirit continues to lovingly comfort and guide us in our daily living.

Love is the great gift God brought to the world through Jesus Christ, and it is exciting because it is the answer to all the problems of life. Does that sound too simple? If people would truly love God with all that they are, if they would love themselves and everyone around them, what problems would continue to exist? Obviously, love includes taking responsibility for economic, environmental, and social issues too. Paying our taxes is also loving our neighbors. Spreading scriptural holiness across the land is the outgrowth of loving churches.

Jesus organized the church through the disciples in order to restore all people to a loving relationship with God. The church is on a mission to help people establish or re-establish a deeper connection with God. Jesus said that the most important task for every human being is to love God with all our heart, soul, and mind. The most important agenda in life is for us to love God with all that we are.

God Wants the Aroma of Love Permeating the Church

Despite the fact that conflicts existed in the early church and have existed in churches of every generation since then, generally the church of God has remained a very loving institution. The letter to the Galatians provides an example of strong conflict in early Christianity. Paul addresses the Galatian Christians as, "You foolish Galatians!" (Gal 3:1) for abandoning life-giving grace in order to live under the oppressive law again. However, with his strong language challenging their behavior, Paul appeals to the Galatians to practice love and writes, "Through love become slaves to one another" (5:13).

The first letter to the Corinthians also deals with conflict. Paul chastises Christians in Corinth for sexual immorality and sinful pride, among other things. However, in the midst of addressing sin in the church, Paul gives us some of the most loving words in all of literature in chapter 13, "Love is patient; love is kind; love is not envious or boastful or arrogant or rude. It does not insist on its own way; it is not irritable or resentful; it does not rejoice in wrongdoing, but rejoices in the truth" (1 Cor 13:4-6).

John appeals to Christians in the early church, "Beloved, let us love one another, because love is from God; everyone who loves is born of God and knows God. Whoever does not love does not know God, for God is love" (1 John 4:7-8). Love originates with God, and as we live in close daily fellowship with God, that love flows through us.

Throughout the two-thousand-year history of the church, generally the presence and sweet aroma of the Holy Spirit have been evident. As people were loved they felt lifted in spirit and supported in their difficulties. Even when people have faltered in their personal lives, when they not only sinned against God, but also deeply hurt family and friends, they have been forgiven. When, by human standards, they did not deserve to be received into the circle of fellowship again, the unconditional love of God was expressed through the acceptance of the loving disciples of Jesus Christ.

A loving church will not necessarily be a growing church. Many congregations pride themselves on getting along well, but they have plateaued in numbers. Although a happy church may not be a growing church, no church can grow without being a loving church. The old adage about flies being drawn to honey and not to vinegar fits the church. People want to be part of a congregation where they see love and joy, but are repelled by negativism and conflict.

Praying Love into a Church

A praying church is generally a loving church. Those, who humble themselves before God in prayer, are more apt to humble themselves before people as well. Prayer chains create links of love. Participants in church prayer chains, where they uphold persons in need, are oil in the machinery of the church. The church functions more effectively, because of these pray-ers and their prayer efforts. The Holy Spirit uses their caring hearts to create a loving atmosphere in the congregation. Having a strong intercessory prayer emphasis in a church saturates the church with a loving spirit. It is very healthy and loving to list names of persons with special needs, asking the congregation to pray for them.

During my fourteen-plus years in my last congregation, we had much prayer emphasis, and I sensed very little conflict in the church. I attributed the absence of conflict to the praying of the congregation. Opening our lives humbly to the movement of the Holy Spirit brings sweetness to the human spirit, which permeates a church.

The Real Meaning of Love

Love has so many definitions. What does it mean? For me, loving someone means to want the best for that person. Love means to sincerely care for another. This makes loving a matter of the will and not feelings. Feelings change and are harder to control, but we all have power over our wills. We control what we want, and every effective pastor wants the very best for every one of her or his people. And loving laity want the best for everyone in their churches.

Marriages have ended because one or both of the parties said, "We fell out of love." If a marriage has a love built on will instead of feeling, a couple cannot fall out of love. One or both spouses may decide to stop loving the other, or they may say we want the best for each other, but we no longer want to be married. But their decision is a matter of will not feeling.

When Jesus said we ought to love our neighbors, he meant that we should want what is best for them. Neighbors include strangers, and we can want the best for strangers. If love were a matter of feeling, it would be impossible to know how we feel about people we do not know.

Loving people, wanting the best for them, is different from liking them. Even though we must love everybody, we do not need to like everyone. Liking has an emotional component to it. Some people are difficult to like. They may be depressed and always filled with negative speech. A positive word seldom crosses their lips. Even though we may not like them or want to spend a lot of time with such persons, they are deeply loved by God, and Jesus commands us to love and care deeply for them as well. We must want their best and do what is in our power to provide them with compassionate care. True disciples of Jesus Christ love everybody.

Creating a Loving Environment

The pastor as the leader sets the tone for the church. A happy, loving, positive pastor will create a church with the same spirit. Not every pastor has a bubbling personality, but every pastor can be loving to all of his or her people.

The most important phrase a pastor can use to create a feeling of being loved is "thank you." Every task in a church is a loving task. When people give a part of themselves for the work of Jesus Christ, the leadership of the church wisely says, "Thank you." When people are appreciated for self-giving, it contributes to the spirit of love within a congregation.

Offering Relational Opportunities

What practical ways are there to enhance the love environment in a church? Food has been used by God throughout the ages. In the book of Acts, Luke tells us of the early church eating together. "Day by day, as they spent much time together in the temple, they broke bread at home and ate their food with glad and generous hearts, praising God and having the goodwill of all the people. And day by day the Lord added to their number those who were being saved" (2:46-47). In these passages Luke connects the love, joy, and good will shown in the group to how that attitude attracts others.

People saw what was happening among those Christians, and they wanted to be part of that loving environment. The opportunities for parishioners to enjoy food together are endless. Wednesday evening church meals, church picnics, stewardship dinners, periodic potluck dinners, or dinners for eight in private homes are only a few possibilities. One of the indicators of a healthy church is when members spend time together during the week, just to enjoy one another.

Members in churches of all sizes need opportunities to get acquainted and to have fellowship. Persons in very small and, particularly, rural churches generally know one another fairly well, but still need opportunities to build joyous relationships. What other interests, besides sharing a meal, can you use to get people together?

Sports are of interest to the vast majority of Americans. Go to ball games together. This will be one way to encourage more men to get involved in the church, as men are generally very sports minded. However, many women enjoy sports as well. If your church is within an hour or two of a major city, organizing a bus ride to see a professional basketball, baseball, or football game can be a lot of fun. We used to rent an elementary school gym on Friday nights to have church volleyball.

Hayrides for couples or families give people an opportunity to develop loving relationships. A hayride under a star-studded sky with a full moon is a lot of fun for a church family.

The serious-minded pastor who thinks these fun times are a waste of time because "they are not spiritual" is wrong. Letting people relate to one another and develop their relationships is as important to the health of a church as are prayer meetings. God uses fun-loving gatherings to help build the church.

Dealing with Conflict

How do you deal with conflict? I don't know anybody who finds it easy to deal with. My experience has been that conflict in meetings can usually be talked through. Disagreements on worship, staffing, organizational, building, or budget matters involve a lot of healthy discussion. Although not every person can be fully pleased, generally we arrive at a consensus.

The most difficult conflicts are often between laypeople. When laity become upset and say hurtful words to each other, how can the pastor help? Naturally, the pastor can and should listen to each one, if he or she learns about the conflict. The pastor may be able to help the laypeople understand one another better, and that may soften the pain.

Asking the people in conflict to get together on their own may work. Perhaps getting the people together in a social setting may help. Sometimes people can make an effort to show respect for one another even though they may never like one another. They can still work and worship together out of mutual respect.

However, there are times when, no matter how much the pastor tries to bring reconciliation, it does not work. Wonderful members leave for other congregations because they are deeply offended by other laypersons. It hurts the pastor and the church, but the pastor simply needs to accept that as part of life.

Pastors can be targets of frustration or anger from parishioners. How do you get over your anger and irritation? Negative attitudes and emotions are hard to overcome. How do you develop positive feelings toward someone who has hurt you? How can you stop that person from popping into your mind, constantly interrupting your thoughts, your work, and your relationships?

Two decades ago I developed a meditation process for overcoming negative feelings toward people. When I was hurt by someone and wanted to be free from it, I would go into a room and sit in a comfortable chair. Alone, I would close my eyes and envision that person doing what he or she liked most. While keeping a happy image of that person, I would pray repeatedly, "Lord Jesus Christ, bless (the name of the one who hurt me)." The sweet movement of the Holy Spirit would melt cold feelings and give me a spirit of peace about that person. God has used that process many times to help me be the loving person I want to be. I recommend this for a five-minute experience. This process has been shared with countless people in counseling over the years, and they have expressed their gratitude.

Laughter in the Hallways

A loving church is usually a happy church. People enjoy one another; they joke and laugh together. When the corridors of the church ring with laughter, that is a sign of a healthy church. A wall plaque says, "Joy is the only infallible sign of a Christian." Joy is certainly reflected in a congregation that is well.

Discussion questions

1. What can we do to raise the love spirit in our church?
2. What kinds of dinners can we offer at the church?
3. What kinds of dinners can we organize for homes?
4. How can we increase the number of sports, theater, and picnic outings for our people?
5. What kind of sporting activities can we offer our people, where they can play softball, volleyball, basketball, or other kinds of games together?
6. How can we bring more laughter into our church?

5

Witness: Stirring Up More Gossiping of the Gospel

Who helped you put your faith in Jesus Christ? Whom did God use to touch your life for Jesus Christ? Were your parents your first and primary witnesses for Christ? Or was it a pastor, Sunday school teacher, or friend? *You believe because of someone else's witness.*

Indeed, God uses the lives of many people to win one person to faith in Jesus Christ. Bob Tuttle, a professor of evangelism, tells of feeling great about leading a man to put his faith in Jesus Christ. Then he read that it takes twenty-five people to lead someone to Christ, and it deflated his spirit. Many people have touched you and me in our faith journey.

Few Evangelists but All Witnesses

Evangelism is a spiritual gift, but being a witness to our experiences of Christ is an expectation. God wants us to share our stories. Luke tells us that the risen Christ told his disciples, "You will receive power when the Holy Spirit has come upon you; and you will be my witnesses in Jerusalem, in all Judea and Samaria, and to the ends of the earth" (Acts 1:8). Jesus was addressing not only his immediate disciples, but disciples of all generations: "You will be my witnesses."

The early church witnessed to the wonder found in Jesus Christ, and that is the reason two billion people on earth today walk by faith in

Christ. For the early church, the apostle Paul was a preeminent witness to Christ's saving power, and the book of Acts tells of Paul's missionary journeys. Paul wrote, "I pray that the sharing of your faith may become effective when you perceive all the good that we may do for Christ" (Phlm v. 6).

Sharing our faith is God's idea, but it is such a wonderful story from a human standpoint that we want to tell it. We have a loving, seeking, and saving God, who came to us in Jesus Christ to restore us to the wonderful life that Adam and Eve had in the garden. This is such an amazing story that it has to be told. Paul says it well in his letter to the Christians in Rome: "For while we were still weak, at the right time Christ died for the ungodly. Indeed, rarely will anyone die for a righteous person—though perhaps for a good person someone might actually dare to die. But God proves his love for us in that while we still were sinners Christ died for us" (5:6-8).

Even though we have all sinned and fallen short of the glory of God, God loves us as children. God came to us in Jesus Christ to lift us and redeem us. Through faith in Jesus Christ we are restored to a loving relationship with God.

Because of this glorious love of God, we are compelled to share our faith. Paul writes in his second letter to the Christians in Corinth, "For the love of Christ urges us on, because we are convinced that one has died for all; therefore all have died" (5:14).

God needs the loving witness of Christians in order to win the world to Christ. God wants the people living with freedom in Christ to help others get out of their self-centered prisons. Paul writes, "And he died for all, so that those who live might live no longer for themselves, but for him who died and was raised for them" (2 Cor 5:15). The world thinks that living for self is the greatest expression of freedom but doesn't realize that living that way means being imprisoned in a very small self. Christians know that real freedom comes by losing one's self by faith in Christ.

Out of our love for others, we want to share how they can find this freedom in Christ. Life is hard, and for many people it is also boring and meaningless. The power of the Holy Spirit has come upon us to share with people in order that they can become new persons in Christ. Paul again writes, "So if anyone is in Christ, there is a new creation: everything old has passed away; see everything has become new!" (2 Cor 5:17).

A New Creation Story

Jain was raised in a non-Christian home, where her mother and grandmother lived their lives with the use of tarot cards. Now married with two children at the age of thirty, she had made some bad choices. She was miserable, lying in her second-floor bed one night, so she called out to God in desperation, and God answered her. She was flooded with this beautiful, sweet, overwhelming emotion, but she did not understand what happened. She felt a need to talk with someone who could give her insight into her experience. It was summertime, and the next morning as she drove to find a church in order to talk with a pastor about her experience, not only was she a new creation, but the earth was new. She said the flowers were more colorful, the trees were greener, and the sky was bluer. Everything was new.

The most amazing thing we have to tell is that we mere human beings can actually become sons and daughters of the creator of the universe. The one who created a hundred billion galaxies, each with one hundred billion stars, is willing to have a personal, intimate relationship with us, so we can not only call him Father, but also Abba, Daddy.

Paul says it this way, "All this is from God, who reconciled us to himself through Christ, and has given us the ministry of reconciliation; that is, in Christ God was reconciling the world to himself, not counting their trespasses against them, and entrusting the message of reconciliation to us" (2 Cor 5:18-19). Because we are now reconciled with God as daughters and sons, God expects us to tell the story. Paul continues, "So we are ambassadors for Christ, since God is making his appeal through us; we entreat you on behalf of Christ, be reconciled to God" (2 Cor 5:20).

Much to Be Excited About

God is so wonderful, and receiving the grace of God is so amazing, that we Christians have a lot to talk about. I have always been excited about Jesus Christ, and as I grow older the excitement increases. Why am I excited? Because of what God does for people at every level of life. First, it is exciting for individuals. Countless people are finding strength for daily living through their faith. Persons filled with guilt, because of having made bad choices, are finding new inner peace through the cleansing work of Jesus Christ on the cross. The sick are finding hope and healing through the Great Physician. Those struggling for direction are finding guidance through the Holy Spirit.

Second, it is exciting to see what God does for marriages. Husbands and wives who are open to the grace of God find greater joy in their relationship. In many seminars across America, I have asked people to raise their hand if they are married. Then I asked how many of those who had raised their hand felt that God was important to their marriages. Almost every hand went up again, indicating that Jesus Christ was very important to the health of their marriages.

I have a daughter and son-in-law in the Midwest, who run a small group meeting of Christian couples. During one of my visits to their home, the group met on a Sunday evening, and they invited me to sit in on it. They were finishing a book titled *How to Build Self-Esteem in Your Mate.* Midway through the meeting we men went out to meet in the yard, while the women stayed in the living room. It was deeply inspiring to hear these young husbands talk about how they could love their wives more. A serious faith in Jesus Christ causes husbands and wives to want to serve each other and be most loving. A friend was touched by God in a most unusual way, which caused him to write these loving words to his wife:

> How have you been able to live with me for forty-three years after the way I have treated you? Let me count the ways. Self-righteousness and judgment have led the way, and under these conditions you have survived and continued to love me. I ran you out of the small group I was leading. I quit one of the activities you loved—singing in the choir— and then I complained that we were leading separate lives.

God prompts these kinds of loving expressions in order to heal relationships and strengthen the bonds of marriage.

Third, God does wonders for parents who seek God's help in guiding their children. God does not drop a childrearing manual from heaven for new parents, and raising a child takes enormous strength, wisdom, and work. Jesus Christ has answers for parents who are diligently seeking grace to raise their children.

Fourth, Jesus Christ changes societies. Jesus taught that love is the most important quality in life. Beginning with God and self, God's children are to love their neighbors in the same way. Love means living honestly in our dealings and truthfully in our words. Loving God means being moral sexually. We lay down our lives in service for humanity when we love as Jesus our Lord loved. This type of love produces the most fulfilling life.

Helping People See Excitement in Their Own Stories

Every Christian has a story to tell of how she or he came to know Jesus Christ as Savior and Lord. How do we help our people understand their stories? Can it happen without their talking about them? We understand our experiences most fully when we have opportunity to express them.

How and where can you help your people reflect on their experiences with Christ? When a group gathers for any reason, it is appropriate to talk about experiences with Jesus Christ. Every group meeting in a church should have some component of spirituality. This is true not only for Bible studies or prayer groups but also for finance or trustees meetings that deal with stewardship of church funds and the church building.

Books have been written protesting deadly, boring meetings, but God will enliven and inspire meetings where people share the reason for their being involved—their faith in Jesus Christ. People attend church meetings because of their faith in Jesus Christ. It is not only appropriate for people to talk about their faith experiences but also enjoyable and inspiring to hear and support one another as they briefly share their faith journey.

Questions to Help People Understand Their Stories

There are many discussion questions that could be used in meetings to help people better understand their faith and learn to express it more freely. Such discussion starters or questions could be:

1. Share a moment when you felt close to God.
2. What persons were most instrumental in your believing in

Jesus Christ, and how did they influence you? What were the times and circumstances?

3. When did you become a Christian, and how did it happen?
4. Paul had an instantaneous conversion, but most people have a more gradual experience in coming to Christ. How did it happen to you?
5. Why do you believe in Jesus Christ today? What difference does Jesus make in your life? In your marriage, family, work, or community? How would your life be different without Jesus Christ?
6. Have you recently been blessed as you gave yourself in ministry either to an individual or a group? If serving Jesus brings you fulfillment, how does that happen, and what kind of fulfillment do you receive?
7. How has the Holy Spirit moved in your life recently, either in worship or private prayer? Or, how does God touch your life, generally, in worship or in private prayer?
8. Tell how you talked with someone outside our church about your faith in Jesus Christ, or tell how you invited someone to come to worship with you recently.

If church members were regularly given opportunities to talk about such questions, God could bring new energy to a church.

Stories of Witness in Scripture

The New Testament reflects a variety of ways that people came to Christ in the early church. In some cases it was family. Paul reminded Timothy that through his maternal grandmother, Lois, and his mother, Eunice, he turned to Christ (2 Tim 1:3-5). From the time he was a little boy his mother and grandmother taught him how to pray. They taught him little choruses and Bible stories. Together they went to someone's home where they had regular Sunday worship. Eunice probably prayed with Timothy before they ate and also in the evening before bed.

Do you still have children at home with you? I hope you take advantage of not only praying before you eat but also using devotional guides like the *Upper Room* with your family. Have someone read the scripture, someone else read the story, and then pray together. It is a great gift to share our faith with our children. Encourage your families to do this.

Andrew gives us an illustration of one sibling witnessing to another. Andrew apparently had been a disciple of John the Baptist, but when John directed him to Jesus, he began following him. After spending some time with Jesus, Andrew got his brother, Simon, and brought him to Jesus (John 1:35-42). Andrew had been touched by Jesus, and wanted his brother, Simon, to meet this special man. Andrew didn't have a clue that his brother would become the leader of the Jerusalem church after Jesus was crucified. Do you have brothers and sisters who are not walking with God? Who are not worshiping Jesus Christ? Jesus needs us to help love our siblings and bring them to faith in him.

Philip gives us an example in scripture, where a friend witnesses to a friend.

> The next day Jesus decided to go to Galilee. He found Philip and said to him, "Follow me." Now Philip was from Bethsaida, the city of Andrew and Peter. Philip found Nathanael and said to him, "We have found him about whom Moses in the law and also the prophets wrote, Jesus son of Joseph from Nazareth." Nathanael said to him, "Can anything good come out of Nazareth?" Philip said to him, "Come and see." When Jesus saw Nathanael coming toward him, he said of him, "Here is truly an Israelite in whom there is no deceit!" (John 1:43-47)

These words from Jesus are some of the most wonderful words anyone could say about you or me: The King James Bible says, "In whom is no guile."

Note three things about Philip's witness. First, he was convinced that he found the one who could bring new life. He believed Jesus was unique and could help people with life. Second, he went out and found a friend; he wanted to share that faith with someone else. Third, even when his friend was skeptical, he did not give up. Our friends may be skeptical about our witness, and they may reject what we say. But continuing to love them is the way of God.

When we witness to others, there is nothing wrong with admitting faith struggles. In fact it will likely help people to know that you were vulnerable in your faith development. Even though Peter comes across in the book of Acts as a macho Christian, someone who is wonderfully strong and certain about faith, it was not always that way. Peter was likely among the disciples who argued about which of them would be considered the greatest. He challenged Jesus to allow him to walk on water, and then cried out to be saved when he realized he was sinking. The night Peter told Jesus he would never desert him, he denied Jesus three times. But it was this very man who was so weak, who preached the sermon at Pentecost where 3,000 were baptized and were added to the church. Admitting our past failures and struggles can be encouraging to others who are struggling.

Keeping the Fire of Witness Alive

How do we continue to witness for Christ? By continuing to experience Christ. We bubble with joy *about* Jesus when we continue to find joy *in* him. When we experience God's grace and wonder, it oozes out of us, most often without any plan on our part. The Holy Spirit is lovingly spontaneous as we share naturally the glory of God in our lives and in the world.

But spontaneity and fire have to be fueled, just as coal had to be shoveled into the old coal furnaces to keep the fire alive. The best way to find motivation for witnessing and faith-sharing is through prayer. When you and I pray for people, something happens. We are naturally led by the Holy Spirit to reach out to them and care for them. I have a stack of slips about one-quarter to one-half inch deep of people I pray for daily. One slip says "my neighbors." I do not know for sure if any of my neighbors worship on Sunday mornings. No doubt because of my praying, God nudged me to invite four of them to a small group discussion I led on Rick Warren's book, *Purpose Driven Life*. Two came and the other two had a conflict.

There is no better way for you to become motivated to care for others and to share your faith than to pray for them. I beg of you that you pray for the unchurched in your life. Harry Denman said that when he prayed for people or a church, he fell in love with them. By that he meant he cared for them deeply. The biggest question we have to answer is this: How can we ignite the fire of faith in the eyes and hearts of all of us? Does it matter to you and me if people don't know the joy we have in Jesus Christ? Do we love them enough to share Christ with them?

Fueling Witness with Discipline

There is a parallel between sports and spirituality. Michael Jordan was great in games because he was great in practice. His grace and spectacular play, which awed millions around the world, was possible only because of his discipline in practice. Christians will share gracious and spontaneous words about their Savior only as they discipline themselves to have fellowship with him. How do we become disciplined?

In order to win others to Christ, we must have the mind of Christ. Paul wrote, "Let the same mind be in you that was in Christ Jesus, who, though he was in the form of God, did not regard equality with God as something to be exploited, but emptied himself, taking the form of a slave, being born in human likeness" (Phil 2:5-7a). When you and I empty ourselves and care for the salvation of others, then we will touch lives for Jesus Christ. People will walk with him in growing numbers, and they will want to be a part of our churches.

But how do we have the mind of Christ? Or, how do we keep our hearts and minds fit, so we will be the most effective witnesses for Christ? Living by the five means of grace as defined by John Wesley is fundamental. God has promised to bless you and me if we regularly practice these five things.

First is fasting, as practiced by the early Christians. The disciples had tried to expel an evil spirit from a boy but failed. Jesus came along and expelled the spirit. Perplexed as to why they had not succeeded, the disciples asked Jesus about this. According to the NRSV footnote regarding some ancient manuscripts' record of Jesus' response, "This kind can come out only through prayer" (Mark 9:29 footnote).

I have been blessed to be able to fast on Tuesdays and Fridays for much of my adult life. I say "blessed" because fasting is possible only by grace. Naturally, it requires discipline and self-denial. Fasting certainly is not a fun experience, but it provides one with joyous, inner strength. I do a liquid fast, so I do not eat solid foods until after 4:00 PM on my fast days.

Second, the reading and study of scripture is important to keep the Christian heart in tune with God. We need to read the objective, written word of God daily. The written word becomes a loving word as the Holy Spirit communicates with our minds and spirits through it.

Third, faithful and humble worship is utterly important. This means worshiping both with the congregation and in private prayer. Worship is utterly important for you and me to remain fit to share our faith in Jesus Christ. In fact, God uses worship services to give you segues to faith-sharing. You may be talking with someone, and something from your pastor's sermon may come to your mind. Sharing your faith naturally will be significantly enhanced if you worship Jesus Christ every week. Through active, personal prayer God enlivens life, so there is much joy and grace to share with others.

Fourth, God promises to bless us as we receive Holy Communion. Our faith is deepened when we receive Jesus Christ anew into our lives through the bread and the cup. John Wesley said Christians should take Holy Communion every opportunity they have.

Last, you remain most fit to be a Christian witness when you participate in a small group. Worship with the congregation provides its own grace, but sharing in a small group is unique. It gives the greatest opportunity to deepen our growth as a Christian. You can develop just as close a relationship to God as Mother Teresa, Billy Graham, and the Pope did. God doesn't listen to any one of them more than God listens to you. We have equal access to God. Nobody on earth has any more access to God than you have. Nobody is any more special to God than you are. God listens to all of God's children equally. As we get closer to God, our whole lives will be a witness to Jesus Christ.

Allowing People to Tell Their Stories in Worship

Every congregation has people of deep faith who are able to express it. Laity inspire others as they tell their faith stories, not only in private and small groups but also in public during worship. I used to pick certain months to invite laity to give a witness of faith. I would give laity five minutes of the worship service to tell part of their faith story.

I had a form with suggestions for them. They could tell how they came to know Jesus Christ and what a difference he made in their lives. Or they could tell about a particular time in their lives when God made a huge difference in their overcoming a difficult situation. Or they could tell about the meaning of prayer in their lives. These suggestions gave them guidelines for their presentation. Not only was the whole congregation inspired by these stories, but also the laity grew in their ability to articulate their faith.

Discussion questions

1. How can we help our church members to better understand their faith stories?
2. How can we help our people be more excited about their faith?
3. How can we inspire more witnessing through our church?
4. How can we give our people more faith experiences that they will want to share?
5. Will it work to have laity witness to their faith in our worship services? If so, when will we do it?
6. What courses can our church teach on witnessing? Who will do it? When?

Resources

1. Ronald Crandall, *Witness: Exploring and Sharing Your Christian Faith* (Nashville: Discipleship Resources, 2001), ISBN 0881773220, available through: Cokesbury bookstores; or by phone through the Direct Sales line, 1-800-672-1789, or your church's Cokesbury representative, 1-888-294-8674; or by going online to www.cokesbury.com.
2. FRAN Plan: small brochure for people to list a friend, relative, acquaintance, or neighbor who has been unchurched for six months. It is helpful in identifying the unchurched, and it motivates witnessing to them. The brochures are sold in packets of one hundred.
3. Call 1-615-340-7068, or order from Discipleship Resources, 1-800-685-4370 or visit the website: www.upperroom.org/bookstore/description.asp?item_id=155022.

6

Passion: When Fire for Christ Burns in Your Bones

A spiritually healthy church will be focused on spending its energies and resources making disciples of Jesus Christ. A church without a strong spiritual foundation will be focused on itself, and it will be satisfied with maintenance instead of growth.

Vision Sees but Passion Drives

Every church needs to have a vision of what God wants it to do. A vision sees possibilities, but in order for the vision to become a reality, it needs to be driven by passion. A builder may have the finest blueprints for the most gorgeous homes, but unless the carpenters have energy and drive to do the work, those houses will never become realities.

If we are to be effective servants of Jesus Christ, we will have both vision and passion in our ministry. Vision is different from passion. Vision has more to do with goals, plans, and purpose. It has more to do with the head, with our understanding and thinking, and with mission statements. Vision deals with the mind, while passion deals with feelings and the heart. Vision provides ideas and understanding. Passion pushes those ideas. Vision sees possibilities, but passion creates expectations. In *The Passion Driven Congregation*, Kent Millard relates how essential it is for a congregation to have a purpose. You need a mission statement; you have to know what your goal is as a congregation. But, he adds, "A congregation with purpose but no passion has no energy to achieve the goal, and a congregation with passion but no clear sense of purpose has energy but no clear sense of direction and will feel scattered and unfocused."[1] The importance of having a mission statement is to understand your passion and to know your goal in order to keep your energy focused in the right direction.

The same is true for pastors as for congregations. A pastor with a great vision but no passion will have an ineffective ministry. That person will forever be a dreamer without achievement. Similarly, pastors with great passion but without a vision will run helter-skelter, not knowing where they are going or why they are doing certain things. When pastors have God-inspired visions that are driven by a deep compulsion to serve Jesus Christ, then they are capable of infusing their churches with profound passion that will propel them to great change.

Passion drives you. What is deep in your heart that motivates you? What is your passion? Rick Warren, in *The Purpose Driven Life*, asks this question: "What would my family and friends say is the driving force of my life?"[2] In considering Warren's suggestion, someone asked me, "Why ask your family and friends what drives you?" I said that you should ask them, because they can see what you do. What you say drives you may not be what you demonstrate through your actions. Our actions tell people where our interests are. Parishioners can tell what their pastor's passions are by watching what the pastor does and where the pastor spends his or her time.

Passion is contagious. The pastor's passion will become the passion of the congregation. Your people will catch your passion or your lack of it. Your passion for ministry is evident in how you spend your time. People watch how you schedule your life, and where you put your energy. Your personal passion will determine how passionate your leadership is in your church. It all starts with you. When laity see their pastor making sacrifices on their behalf, they also lay down their lives in order to serve Jesus Christ.

Being Inspired by the Circuit Riders

The circuit riders have been a constant motivation for me. "Circuit rider" was a term given to Methodist ministers who traveled from place to place, holding services during the early years of our country. Their fervor to bring people to Jesus Christ and to connect them with the power of God drove them to heroic ministry. Not having the option of riding in comfortable cars with cushioned seats, they rode in the open air on horseback. Because there were no heated or air-conditioned vehicles in that day, they were totally exposed to the elements. They rode horseback in rain, sleet, and snow. Cold or heat did not deter them. Driven by a deep desire to glorify God and bring people to a personal relationship with Jesus Christ, they often died for their faith. It was not uncommon that they died for the cause of Christ before they reached forty years of age.

Your church may have been losing members for years, and you may be discouraged. Instead, be encouraged by the circuit riders. Let their passion become your passion. They knew the power of God to create new possibilities, so they had big dreams. They believed what the angel told Mary when she could not understand her pregnancy, "Nothing will be impossible with God" (Luke 1:37). Do not be afraid to think and dream big, because you have an omnipotent God, who is on your side. You may not be in a place where your small membership church will grow to large numbers, but you can guide the people to become the highest quality congregation, which will enable your church to grow to its highest potential. If you have many unchurched people in your community, then numerical growth is a great possibility.

The United Methodist Church has congregations in more of the 3,143 counties, parishes, and independent cities in the United States than any other denomination. This is due to the Circuit Riders who lovingly laid down their lives taking the gospel of Jesus Christ across our country. The same God who inspired those Circuit Riders is still reaching out to save people today. The same grace that allowed John Wesley to change the religious scene across England God also has available for you and me. Think big, because the fields are white unto harvest where you live. Churches look to their clergy as their visionary leaders.

Passion and commitment go hand in hand. The pastor who is deeply inspired to serve Jesus Christ in the local congregation is going to be committed to Christ and the church. The passionate pastor is a dedicated pastor.

Passion is More than Feelings

Passion involves feelings, but it is more than a feeling. It is a drive deep within us that produces not only a strong determination or a wanting but also a powerful will that overrules feelings in life. Our drive or determination helps us control what we want, whereas controlling our feelings or emotions is harder to manage.

Although feelings are involved with passion, it is a mistake to identify passion only as feelings. Feelings take us on a roller coaster ride. Hopefully, the times of feeling great in our ministry are more numerous than the times of feeling down. However, we will faithfully push ahead to make disciples of Jesus Christ, even when we don't feel like it, because we truly have a deep yearning to bring others to Christ.

There is a parallel between passion in ministry and love in marriage. A married couple who considers love to be only a feeling will find their level of love constantly floating up and down. Whereas a couple who believes that real love is a matter of wanting the best for each other can have a very steady love relationship. It is because wanting involves controlling our intentions, whereas feelings involve our emotions. Feelings can have ups and downs like a roller coaster ride, whereas a couple's desire for the best for each other can remain unshaken. A husband or wife can say with integrity, "I will always want the best for you," whereas saying, "I will always feel good about you," is much harder to say, because emotions may fluctuate. Passion in the ministry is the same. A pastor can say, "I will always want the best for my church and our people," even though he or she may not always feel on top of the world about the church.

When Your Passion Doesn't Fit Your Job

Pastoral ministry has many facets to it, including preaching, pastoral work, evangelism, administration, and teaching. Within these areas you have counseling, visitation, supervising, recruiting, and so forth. Few pastors are great at each of these facets of ministry.

Usually we are most passionate about the things that are our strengths. If we truly enjoy preaching, then sermon preparation will be enjoyable for us. The pastor who loves administrative work will spend a lot of time in the office on organizational matters. We tend to spend the bulk of our time at what we enjoy the most. Because it takes more discipline to focus on those things we enjoy less, we tend to spend less time on them. We are less enthusiastic about the work that is more difficult, where we feel less skilled and less comfortable.

So, how do we deal with those tasks in ministry that are not fun for us but are a lot of work? How do we find success in our areas of incompetence? In some instances you can get help from the laity. If administration is not your thing, you may have laypersons gifted with administrative skills who can pick up the slack for you. This may also be true in the areas of teaching, visitation, and counseling. However, what do you do when you are not passionate about preaching? Since no layperson can do that for you, try to find a kind of preaching that excites you. If you have not tried speaking from a manuscript, perhaps you should give that a try. Or, perhaps you are most comfortable speaking from an outline. As preaching is central to your work, there is no way to get anyone else to do it for you. Work at it until you become comfortable with it, and then perhaps God will put passion into your heart for it. Also, pray deeply about it.

Can Passion Be Developed?

Early in my ministry I was very excited about theology and biblical studies. I had no interest or ability in administration, nor did I see its importance in the local church. Most clergy who attended seminary were not trained in administrative work. I was one of them. I had no passion for it; in fact, I had an intense dislike for it.

Then I read an article that said if you dislike administrative work, become good at it. Develop your administrative skills so you will become more proficient at it. Over the years I began to see the utter importance of having a well-organized church, and I learned how to make that happen. Then I developed an excitement about administration; a genuine passion was developed.

What Can Sustain Passion?

Nothing can create excitement like success. Passion grows when worship attendance is strong or growing, when new people keep showing up in worship, and when people are bubbling with enthusiasm about their church. Enthusiasm bursts forth when people are excited about their personal growth, when new study groups develop, and when mission teams return from deeply fulfilling trips. Passion deepens when finances are running strong, when the trustees have to figure out how to create more room for the overflowing Sunday school classes, and when that growing youth group wants its own room. These events boost passion, and passion begets more passion.

However, how do you maintain passion when church life is either blasé or on a downward spiral? How do you remain motivated when the future looks bleak? Think about your calling. Why did you enter the pastoral ministry? To what did God call you? What is more important in ministry than making disciples of Jesus Christ? If this is your motivation for ministry, then there is always work to be done, and you please God when you are passionate about doing that work.

This desire to bring people to Jesus Christ, to find personal and family wholeness in Christ, and to help God make society well has driven me throughout my ministry. After I was ordained in Mandan, North Dakota, at the age of twenty-five, the mother of one of my college friends came through the receiving line. She said, "Royal, I hope you will save many people." She knew that I can't save anybody, but she hoped I would make myself available to God in order to let Christ save people through me. She had a vision that I would be involved in bringing people to a personal relationship with Jesus Christ. That simple conversation helped stimulate me to try to reach people for Christ throughout the years, and reaching people for Christ happens primarily through love.

Passion is strengthened or weakened by personal peace and happiness. Therefore, keeping the home fires burning brightly and making sure everything is in good shape at home is important. Commitment to Jesus Christ can either be enhanced or diverted by family situations. Passionate pastors realize they are most efficient and effective when they are emotionally well. And in order to be emotionally whole, they understand that having loving and smooth family relationships is important. Therefore, passionate pastors give time to their spouse and to their children. Having a loving spouse and happy children often helps pastors fulfill their vision and carry out their passions. The unfortunate corollary is that many clergy are emotionally troubled, because they have not given their spouse adequate time of love and support. Emotional turmoil can create lethargy in a pastor's heart.

God Sustains Passion through a Devotional Life

Vision and passion do not come out of an empty spiritual life. Clergy who are in tune with God are also most in tune with themselves, their families, and with the laity. The Holy Spirit, the great Counselor, gives them new insight as they let God's word filter through their minds and hearts daily. When they are open to Jesus Christ, they receive vision for their work.

Vision and passion are nurtured by a devotional life. Effective pastors take time to commune with God. They set aside a time to be with God, allowing God to talk with them as they open the scriptures and meditate on them. As Martin Luther, John Wesley, and all the great leaders of the church have needed time with God in prayer, so do you and I.

I lost Rita, my wonderful wife of thirty-nine years, in 2002. Two years later I met Evelyn, a devout disciple of Jesus Christ, who has the same moral values that I have, and we got married a year later. During our time of getting acquainted and courting, we worked through a book titled *Before You Remarry*. One chapter deals with making a vision statement. Evelyn and I have written a vision statement for our marriage that goes like this: "We will center our lives on God, while serving Jesus Christ as our Savior and Lord and giving ourselves in service to his church. We will love each other deeply to help each other become the best people we can be, and we will pray for our children daily and help them emotionally and financially as we are able." That is the head stuff, which is good but inadequate by itself. We believe having daily devotions with God at 6:30 AM gives us the passion to live up to that vision statement. That provides the heart stuff.

Linking Our Passion with Saints of the Past

Your call and mine arise out of callings from our past. In Genesis we read: "Now the Lord said to Abram, 'Go from your country and your kindred and your father's house to the land that I will show you'" (12:1). Abraham didn't have a clue as to where he was going, but he was willing to leave his family, his home in Haran, and his country in order to follow the call of God.

When God saw the Israelites suffering in Egypt, God said to Moses, "So come, I will send you to Pharaoh to bring my people, the Israelites, out of Egypt" (Exod 3:10). Although feeling totally incapable of doing the job, Moses obeyed God. The bush that God used to call Moses is still burning today as God calls you to bring people out of slavery to sin and self.

Isaiah was living in a time of social degradation, very much like today's society, when the people called evil good and good evil, darkness light and light darkness. God needed someone to call the people into account. Isaiah said, "Then I heard the voice of the Lord saying, 'Whom shall I send, and who will go for us?' And I said, 'Here am I; send me!'" (Isa 6:8).

Finally, remember the story of God taking Ezekiel through the Valley of Dry Bones as we discussed earlier in chapter 2. Reread Ezekiel 37:1-9 and think about your belief that God can make dry bones come to life again. God gave Ezekiel a vision of new possibilities. Believe that God can bring new life to your church. I encourage you to continue to trust that God is able to redeem people's lives by faith in Jesus Christ. Claim your faith and believe that God can bring new life to individuals; God can restore marriages; God can create new joy in families, and God can make dead churches vital again.

Discussion questions

1. What is my favorite part of ministry?
2. How does my passion support my vision in daily and weekly work? If they don't match, how can I make them match?
3. Is there anything in my life that is hindering my passion? If so, how can I let God get rid of it?
4. What changes in my life would enhance my passion for Christ, his people, and his church?
5. How can I help God bring more passion in my church for Christ, his people, and his church?

Notes

1. E. Carver McGriff and M. Kent Millard, *The Passion Driven Congregation* (Nashville: Abingdon Press, 2003), 56.
2. Rick Warren, *The Purpose Driven Life* (Grand Rapids: Zondervan, 2002), 35.

7

Prayer: Being on Your Knees Can Help You Walk on Air

The life and health of a church are directly proportional to the prayer life of the congregation. The praying church is the healthiest church. When parishioners spend time in prayer, they are a more compassionate and happier people. Their spirit permeates the congregation. When people spend time in communion with God, the sweetness of the Holy Spirit radiates throughout the church.

The pastor is strengthened by the prayers of the congregation. The apostle Paul wrote to the Christians in the city of Corinth that his ministry was blessed by their prayers. He wrote, "as you also join in helping us by your prayers" (2 Cor 1:11a).

God loves your church more than you do, and prayer is a basic way of letting God bless your congregation. God wants your church to be the best it can be, but how can that happen? It may seem simplistic, but our wonderful God has told us, "Ask, and it will be given you; search, and you will find; knock, and the door will be opened for you" (Matt 7:7).

A young salesman in my last church developed the practice of praying for his clients before he called on them. He told me that things went so wonderfully for him that he almost felt guilty. I told him not to feel guilty about praying for his customers, because this is the way God works. Prayer is a way of opening up the heavens and letting grace and mercy come down upon us. Jesus knew that and spent much time in prayer. The gospel writer Luke mentions Jesus praying more than any of the other writers.

The Amazing Gift of Prayer

Prayer is one of the greatest gifts God has given to us. It is an incredible grace to be able to talk with the creator of the world. We used to think that the Milky Way was the only galaxy, and that it had a limited number of stars. But the Hubble telescope has given us amazing vision into the depth of the universe. It is beyond our understanding how God not only created these unfathomable galactic wonders but also designed their beautiful order. Our minds cannot comprehend having the privilege of personally talking with the One who created all that wonder. What an astounding invitation God has given us, to have these personal conversations on a daily basis. This awesome gift is beyond our grasp intellectually but so real experientially, and we are humbled by this privilege.

But having fellowship with God is not all. We have the opportunity to not only talk with Jesus but also listen to him as he talks with us and blesses us. God ministers to us and through us in a quiet, yet powerful manner. God does this to help us with our churches. The Lord wants to help you and your church, and being disciplined to talk with God daily is a basic avenue through which God will offer help.

Prayer as Receiving God's Grace

How we perceive prayer is very important, because it will make us either want to pray or turn away from it. Some people look upon prayer as something they ought to do. What will motivate people to pray more? Will it be the idea that prayer is a duty or a gift?

Imagine a daughter, Jackie, away from home as a freshman in college. Her parents tell her to be sure to call home every two days to let them know how she is. Calling her parents is easy the first few weeks of school. She has lots of time as she has made few friends, and no serious homework has been assigned yet. However, two months into the school year her life has changed. She is busy attending classes, reading textbooks, and writing papers. She also has a very active social life. It is hard for her to find time to call home. It is a pain for her to have to check in with her parents every two days. Don't they know she is now a grown-up? Calling home for Jackie is a duty.

But, let's suppose that Jackie has run out of money. Paying for pizza to be delivered to her dorm in order to share with friends, plus going out on weekends has depleted her resources. Her parents invite her to call anytime she needs to bolster her bank account. Now Jackie can't wait to call home. She needs help and knows that her loving parents will bail her out. Calling home out of duty compared to calling in order to receive something changes her attitude completely.

Which image fits our reason for praying to God? One of the most important things to remember is that prayer is an act of grace. It is allowing God to love us and to give us divine goodness. Someone once compared praying to turning on an electric switch. Turning on the switch does not create the current but does provide a channel through which the electric current may flow.

Prayer, indeed, is God's way of blessing us. Taking time to pray to Jesus lets him love us. Prayer is a love experience. When we humbly focus on God, grace floods the soul, and the Holy Spirit moves upon us in a glorious way. We are all unique and relate to God differently. The Holy Spirit has graced me many times with new ideas, and Jesus has given me more new thoughts during prayer than I can remember.

Jesus Prayed about His Life and Work

Jesus spent much of his time praying in the wilderness before beginning his ministry. Luke writes about Jesus' ministry, "But now more than ever the word about Jesus spread abroad; many crowds would gather to hear him and to be cured of their diseases" (Luke 5:15). What does that mean? Jesus was swamped with work! People were coming to him asking for help. How did he respond? Luke continues, "But he would withdraw to deserted places and pray" (Luke 5:16). He needed strength from God in order to do his work, because even though he was God, he was also man. He had to learn how to deal with all this attention and how to handle his work.

Jesus sought God's wisdom before he chose the disciples. Luke wrote that the day before he chose his disciples, Jesus "went out to the mountain to pray; and he spent the night in prayer to God" (Luke 6:12). Jesus knew that leadership is everything in life, and it was very important that he pick the right people to found the church.

In other places such as chapter 9 verse 28 and chapter 11 verse 1, Luke writes that Jesus, in the midst of ministry, went off to be by himself to pray. No doubt he prayed to stay in touch with God and to pray about his work.

Facing trial and death, Jesus wanted to be alone with God. On the night when he was betrayed, he took his disciples to the Mount of Olives. He had gone there often to pray, and this place was of particular importance on this night. Facing death, he went to a very familiar spot where he sought the help of God more than ever before. Luke tells us that on the night Jesus was betrayed, "He came out and went, as was his custom, to the Mount of Olives; and the disciples followed him" (Luke 22:39).

What can we learn from Jesus' prayer life? First, as God loved Jesus deeply and helped him, so God loves you dearly and wants to help your church. Second, to accept God's love through daily, regular prayer is to accept a gift. Third, God wants to help you with your decisions, your important choices. Finally, when things get tough, know that God stands with you, and spend extra time in prayer.

Organizing a Personal Prayer Team

Clergymen and clergywomen across America are developing their own prayer teams. I recruited six male friends and colleagues, asking them to pray for me. Four are local, and two live out of state. It is my habit to e-mail them weekly with my prayer needs. I ask them to pray mainly for my work; but if something personal arises, I seek their prayers for that as well. Naturally, it requires openness on my part to share my needs. God has infused me with grace and strength from the daily prayers of these men. I have been encouraged, motivated, strengthened, and inspired by them.

In return, I am blessed as I pray for them. As I send my needs, I request that they let me know how I can pray for them. My daily schedule involves my being in my office at seven o'clock in the morning. My first act is to kneel and pray for each of these prayer partners and their needs. This daily prayer time has provided a very inspiring relationship with these men in addition to the weekly prayers and support.

If you are a clergyperson or layperson, I recommend that you organize your own prayer team, whether it has two, three, or six persons. Make a covenant to pray for each other daily, and then share your needs with each other. It is a simple but powerful experience to inform your team about your prayer needs each week and then to ask them to also keep you informed of their needs. God will bless your life and your ministry through this experience of being lifted up before God, daily, by others. The Holy Spirit provides profound support in one's daily life as others lift you and your work before God in prayer on a regular basis. Encourage your laypeople to organize their own prayer teams. Jesus will infuse your church with new life if it is filled with praying people.

America would become a gloriously different country if there were hundreds of thousands of prayer teams across our nation. It would truly spread "scriptural holiness" across our land.

Asking the Congregation to Pray for You

Pastors who ask their congregations to pray for them create a large reservoir of grace and support. Some people find it very easy to say, "Pray for me." I have not been one of them, but I wish that I had asked for the prayers of my congregations. Several very positive things happen when clergy ask their congregations to pray for them. First, they have the gift of being lifted before God by their people, so they are directly blessed by our Lord. Second, by asking for prayers, they express a very healthy vulnerability. Parishioners identify with a pastor who shows personal need. Third, God creates a more loving bond between parishioners and their pastor when there is mutual prayer support.

A pastor in the Northwest in the late 1980s was experiencing conflict in his church. There was dissention and anger. After attending a prayer workshop in 1989, the pastor made a concerted effort to make his church a praying congregation. He organized prayer vigils; he asked each church member to form a seven-member prayer team. And he asked each member of the congregation to pray for him each month on the day of their birth. For example, someone who was born on July 10 would pray for the pastor on the tenth day of each month.

What happened to that church? The icy strife was melted away by the warmth of the Holy Spirit. As loving prayers replaced griping and criticism, love gradually moved throughout the church. Along with love came beautiful change. In a community of just 1800 people, worship attendance rose from 180 to 600 in just three years after this focus on prayer.

Setting the Prayer Tone of the Church

As in everything else in the church, the pastor sets the tone. Everything starts at the top, even in prayer. People look to the pastor as their model, and the pastor's life inspires the lives of the parishioners. Pastors can look upon this as a wonderful privilege rather than a great burden.

Yes, laity also have great influence. Some lay prayer warriors are of great inspiration to a congregation. Although the pastor is to set the example for the church, lay people have as much access to the heart of God as pastors have. Any layperson can get just as close to Jesus Christ as any ordained clergy. Congregations are blessed by their praying laypersons.

Pastors Teach Empowering Prayer

As the pastor models prayer for the congregation, the pastor also has the honor of teaching the congregation about prayer. The disciples did not know much about prayer, so one of them asked Jesus, "Lord, teach us to pray, as John taught his disciples" (Luke 11:1). Laypersons also wish to learn and need to be taught how to pray.

Every pastor will enrich his or her parishioners' lives by teaching them the five elements of prayer: praise, thanksgiving, confession, intercession, and petition.

Praise is the highest form of prayer, because it is the most unselfish. The Psalmist wrote, "Praise the LORD! Praise the LORD, O my soul! I will praise the LORD as long as I live; I will sing praises to my God all my life long" (Ps 146:1-2).

To praise God is to acknowledge God for who God is. It is to recognize the Lord's great intelligence and power. In their book *Rare Earth*, Peter D. Ward and Donald Brownlee claim that it is unlikely that intelligent animal life as it is known on earth exists anywhere else in the universe. They say the reason is that the composition and stability of the earth is very uncommon. There is the right amount of oxygen on earth and the exact amount of energy from the sun. Earth has the right balance of land and water to maintain the required temperatures. They also say that without the moon and Jupiter there likely would be no animal life on earth; the moon gives consistency to our seasons by balancing the tilt of the earth.[1]

How does Jupiter protect the earth? Hollywood sells horror movies depicting earth being destroyed by huge objects from outer space. God has protected against that by creating planet Jupiter, which is so big that 1,000 earths could be packed inside it. Being so huge it has enormous gravitational pull, drawing rocks and other objects to itself so that they do not hit the earth. God is so magnificently intelligent and powerful to understand that we would be clobbered by rocks from space, so God put Jupiter as a cosmic vacuum cleaner sucking up debris from outer space in order to protect us. We praise God for being all-powerful.

But we also praise God for being a deeply loving God and for putting up with our selfishness and thoughtlessness. God is worthy of our highest glory just for who God is, totally apart from anything God has done for us.

The second element of prayer is thanksgiving. Here we remember God for what God has done. Paul wrote to the Christians in Colossae, "As you therefore have received Christ Jesus the Lord, continue to live your lives in him, rooted and built up in him and established in the faith, just as you were taught, abounding in thanksgiving" (Col 2:6-7). They thanked God constantly.

The blessings of God that are given to us are abundant and profound. All people can identify with giving thanks for the human body. Pastors can emphasize to their congregations that during one hour of worship God pumps the heart of each worshiper 4000 times. Do you realize that is 96,000 times a day? It is impressive to consider that the human body has 66,000 miles of blood vessels. That is more than twice the number of miles around the middle of the earth. Yet God lovingly and faithfully moves the blood throughout those thousands of miles, feeding the various parts of the body with oxygen.

The number of items for which we can thank God is endless. We could spend our whole lives thanking God and could never cover all the reasons we have to be thankful. The wise pastor will help his or her people to be a thankful people, which will be used by Jesus to help change the congregation, and transform the lives of the laypeople and their families.

Third, we confess our sins to God. John wrote in his first letter, "If we confess our sins, he who is faithful and just will forgive us our sins and cleanse us from all unrighteousness. If we say that we have not sinned, we make him a liar, and his word is not in us" (1 John 1:9-10). When we are honest, we admit to having entertained thoughts we should not have thought, having said words we should not have expressed and having done deeds we ought not to have done. Those are sins of commission.

Then there are sins of omission when we are lazy, leaving undone what we ought to have done. The Holy Spirit calls us into ministries, that would help build the kingdom of God, but we are too engrossed in our own issues to follow that calling. All of us have failed God, and not being loving is basic to our failures. God's perfect standard of love ought to be our standard. Each of us fails this standard constantly.

Fourth, there are prayers of intercession. We have the great privilege of praying for others, lifting them up to God and asking God to bless them. Paul wrote to the Christians in Colossae, "For this reason, since the day we heard it, we have not ceased praying for you and asking that you may be filled with the knowledge of God's will in all spiritual wisdom and understanding" (Col 1:9). One of the great gifts we have is to pray for loved ones and friends in distant places. Through our caring we know that God will respond to our prayers and bless them.

But something else positive happens with a strong intercessory prayer life. Do you know what happens to you when you pray a lot for other people? God makes you a better person. Not only are you a blessing to other people, but also you, yourself, become more loving and gracious.

Last, we petition God, praying for ourselves. Jesus invited us to pray for our personal needs. His invitation to ask, search, and knock is an open invitation with the only qualifier being that you and I pray for that which is God's will. All the wonderful things that make for a full life are included: joy, health, strength, wisdom, safety, housing, and yes, even money.

Loving the Congregation through Prayer

God uses love to create love, and love can be expressed through prayer. Twice a year my wife and I prayed through the entire membership of the church. This may have been done at the beginning of the school year, at the beginning of the New Year, or at Easter. We would name each family and their children before God, asking God to bless them in a special way. Then we would send a card to each family with words such as these:

Dear Bob and Mary,

We lifted you up before God in prayer today asking that God would bless you in a special way. Our prayers were for Jesus Christ to provide you with health and strength, and that all of your life would be well. Thank you for being a member of First Church.
Sincerely,

We personalized these cards by writing in the names. Every time we offered these prayers, people would come through the line on Sunday morning expressing their appreciation for them. Often someone said, "That card came at just the right time." Through these loving intercessions the Holy Spirit moved upon our hearts, giving us a deeper sense of caring for the people. Sweet compassion filled the spirit, expressing itself in greater ministry. Furthermore, when we made it known that we prayed for people, they felt cared for and loved. That spirit of goodwill permeated the congregation. Even though these prayers were simply offered out of genuine love for the members of the church, they had another effect. They enlarged the spirit of love in the church, and that minimized conflict.

Creating a Daily Prayer Time at Your Church

It is a gift to offer your people a daily prayer opportunity. At Friendship Church in Bolingbrook, Illinois, we had a one-hour prayer meeting at six in the morning, from Monday through Friday. It was very informal. We began the time reading Scripture and devotional literature. The praying was mostly intercessory, as we prayed through a stack of cards with prayer requests. During that time we lifted the concerns of people with problems to God, and asked that God would bless them in a special way. Many people came to this early prayer meeting. Some attended simply to participate in prayer. Countless others came on their way to work asking for special grace. Sometimes their prayer needs were job related. Others came with relational problems. Many came with prayer requests related to health concerns.

An early morning prayer meeting allows many people to attend who are employed outside the home, because they can come on their way to work. However, the prayer time could be in the evening when people are at home. Consistency and communication are required to make this work. Somebody has to be there, and there may be an advantage for the pastor to be present. The prayer opportunity has to be constantly publicized so that people are aware of it.

A Program Prayer Group

Churches with strong evangelistic vitality have exciting opportunities for people to grow. God infuses these programs with special grace when they are supported by prayer. First United Methodist Church in Peoria, Illinois, has had such a ministry, where a group prays for everything that happens in the church.

We made the three-hour round trip to Peoria to talk with their prayer leaders and then went home to create our own program prayer group. The group met monthly and created a schedule of areas of the church to lift before God for the next time period. The congregation was asked to pray for particular programs through each newsletter. God used those prayers to enrich the learning, serving, and growing opportunities of the church through the prayers of the congregation.

How Do We Pray?

First, there are arrow prayers, when we mentally shoot arrow prayers to God throughout the day if something happens. You might be driving along when someone comes to mind that is having problems, and you say, "Lord, please bless Jack or Mary in this time of trouble." I find myself often saying, "Thank you, God," after I have completed two sets of exercises on a weight machine at the health club.

Second, there is conversation with God throughout the day. Brother Lawrence, in his little book *Practicing the Presence of God*, made this popular. He had a sense of God's presence with him all the time and had conversations with God throughout each day. Brother Lawrence was Nicholas Herman, who lived in the 1600s. He was a lowly monk who became well known for his saintly spirit. Similarly, Mother Teresa, in our own day, was a very humble, frail woman who caught the imagination of the whole world. Even the rich and powerful wanted to be like her.

Many people talk with God while they drive. You might be going to a meeting, praying for the people involved and for the time to go well. I have been in many meetings when we got stuck, and I would kneel at the altar of my heart and pray the Jesus prayer, "Lord Jesus Christ, have mercy on me. Lord Jesus Christ, have mercy on me." Through that prayer God would keep me focused in the meeting, sometimes giving a creative idea and always making me a more useful participant. Some of you pray while working at the kitchen sink.

Third, there are those of us who set times in the day when we turn to Jesus Christ in a focused manner. For some of us this prayer time is in the early morning; others pray at noon or in the evening. Concentration in prayer is easier in the morning when the mind is most alert. If we wait until we go to bed, often our prayer turns to sleep. It helps to close the eyes to concentrate more deeply, while lifting our thoughts to God. This can happen in a room within your house, or in your office, or in church. To deepen concentration, it may help to pray aloud. God does not need to hear us, but it helps us to hear ourselves. We can concentrate better when we hear our own voices. Even the sound of a whispered prayer allows us to focus our minds more clearly on our prayers.

A Personal Prayer with Profound Grace

About 1995 we were vacationing in the mountains of northwest North Carolina. I had been taking medication for gastritis but ran out of it. The symptom of severe abdominal pain returned in the middle of the night. I prayed, "Dear God, I love you. Lord Jesus Christ, I love you. Holy Spirit God, I love you," and the pain began subsiding. I prayed again, "Dear God, I love you. Lord Jesus Christ, I love you. Holy Spirit God, I love you," and the pain disappeared. I have prayed that prayer 25,000 times since God healed my body that night.

Our son, Paul, was in a group of young Christian musicians touring Central and South America many years ago. Colombia, at that time, was filled with danger because of the drug traffic. They were met by soldiers, toting automatic rifles, who accompanied them through the airport so that nobody would steal their instruments and sound equipment.

It was an anxious time, but their leader said to them, "The safest place for us to be is in the center of God's will."

Jesus said that the first commandment is to love God with all our heart, mind, soul, and strength. He said that there is nothing more important than loving God. Praying the prayer, "Dear God, I love you. Lord Jesus Christ, I love you. Holy Spirit God, I love you," puts one smack dab in the middle of God's will, which is the safest place on earth. God has calmed my soul countless times in the quiet darkness of the night, and in the hustle of the day as I expressed my life to God with these words.

Discussion questions

1. Would the leadership of our church pray for the entire congregation naming each family? If so, could we send a postcard to each family letting them know we lifted them up before God in loving prayer?
2. What small groups could we offer for studying books on prayer?
3. Does our church have a prayer chain? If not, how could we organize one?
4. Does our prayer chain in the church use the Internet to get out timely e-mail, asking people to pray for members of the church?
5. If no prayer group exists in our church, how could we organize one or more groups, for which there would be specific times and places when members could come to join others in prayer?
6. How could we help persons in our church create their own prayer teams?

Note

1. Peter D. Ward and Donald Brownlee, *Rare Earth* (New York: Copernicus, 2000), 221.

8

Time Management: Getting Twenty-four Hours from Every Day

I was writing a presentation on time management, when I typed into my Internet Explorer the words, "effective use of time." These words popped up on my screen:

> Sooner. Better. More. Now. Yesterday! Can you ever get it all done? The time we spend each day not accomplishing what we want or need to accomplish can add significant stress to our business and personal lives. But since we can't change time, we must learn how to make the most of the time we have. This training program shows how to virtually "add" minutes to each day by forming a logical, prioritized sequence or "plan of action." [1]

The advertisement was for a video titled *Time Challenged*, and the company offered it for sale at $795 or for rent at $225. It was incredible that they wanted so much money for a product that helps people manage their time. However, learning how to manage time is so important that resources for helping people manage their time can bring this kind of money. The advertisement for this video said that helping people with time management also helped them reduce stress. It claimed that people who manage their time most efficiently are the least stressed.

The Incredible Gift of Time

Time is an amazing concept. Outside the love of God in Jesus Christ, time is our most treasured gift. Time is the only resource that we cannot reuse or regain once it is lost. It is our greatest blessing, and for many it is our greatest source of weakness. The unabridged edition of the *Random House Dictionary* says the Achilles' heel is soft. Therefore, it is a spot that is particularly vulnerable. The place most of us are very vulnerable in life is in our management of time. Time management is everyone's Achilles' heel.

Clergy are both blessed and cursed in their time expenditure. On the one hand, we clergy do not punch time clocks, so we have freedom to spend our time as we think most valuable. On the other hand, we wrestle with the use of time, because it requires much thought, prayer, and discipline to use it properly.

We all are blessed with exactly the same amount of time. We all have twelve months in a year, roughly thirty days in a month and seven days in each week. That gives us each one hundred sixty-eight hours in a week, and twenty-four hours each day. So, we are all on the same playing field in terms of time. The president of the United States doesn't have one minute more time than you have, and you have no more time than the homeless person wandering the city streets. We obviously can't change the amount of time we have, so we have to learn to manage our time the best we can.

Planning a Weekly Schedule Is Best

As we plan our lives, what kind of planning is best? Stephen Covey, in his book *First Things First*, writes that weekly planning is most effective.[1] A month is too big a chunk of time to plan. It is too large a slice of pie to handle. There is too much time involved in planning each day for thirty days in advance. In contrast, if you try planning your life on a daily basis, that puts you into a crisis mode, dealing with immediate things all the time.

Covey writes that weekly planning is best because it includes mornings, days, evenings, and weekends. It is the most logical span of time to plan. When I have my schedule worked out for every day, a week in advance, I find much natural motivation in knowing what is coming each day. If I planned only one day at a time, there would not be carry-over motivation but rather anxiety about having to take time to plan daily.

My weekly practice for many years has been to spend a half hour to an hour preparing my schedule for the next week. I usually do it on Sunday afternoon or evening, so on Monday morning I am already anticipating what I am going to be about. When children are told they are going to get a treat, they anticipate it and can wait for it. Adults who plan for activities are also motivated to get to them. Instead of dreading Monday morning, I am full of expectation, looking forward to what the week will bring.

In addition to making out the larger schedule for the week, I also keep tabs on my work through each day. When I am at my computer, I often find it helpful to estimate the amount of time it will take me to complete a task. It helps me stay on target. Usually, if I allow fifteen minutes for a job, it is amazing how often I can finish within those fifteen minutes. When workmen come to your home to fix something, they get a call asking, "How are you coming?" The company thinks they should be able to get that job done within a certain period of time.

Maintaining a Balance

Pastors live enormously complex lives, trying to manage their personal lives and relate to their families, their churches, and their communities. How does a pastor juggle all the roles and responsibilities within a church: administrator, fundraiser, pastor, counselor, preacher, teacher, supervisor, spiritual guide, property manager, and others? Where do you spend your time? How do you determine which of these areas is most important, and how do you allocate time to each of them?

One of the most difficult decisions every person, not just pastors, has to make is to learn when to say no. What are you willing to say "no" to? Isn't it amazing that learning when to say that little two-letter word is both difficult and utterly important?

Hobbies are good and helpful. We need to maintain balance in life. Golf is a very relaxing activity for countless effective pastors. Many clergy enjoy watching sports, comedy, and movies on television. Every clergyperson has to determine how much diversion is needed in order to most effectively serve Jesus Christ.

How much leisure and entertainment is in God's will for you and me? Obviously, every hour spent in front of the television or on the Internet, that is unrelated to our work, takes away an hour from serving Jesus Christ.

How Do the Laity Know That the Pastor Is Working?

A layman once complained to me that he was getting up to leave for work early, while his pastor slept late. This layman apparently felt cheated. He was giving faithfully to the work of Christ in the church, while he thought the pastor was not putting in his time.

Fundamentally, every pastor needs to earn the respect and trust of his or her people in regard to how his or her time is spent. How is that respect earned? It is earned when laity see effective leadership in the church. Pastors gain respect when laity experience inspiring worship, when they see new people coming to worship, when they delight in deeper learning experiences, and when they are touched by participating in mission experiences. Trust is developed when the pastor visits the sick, makes caring telephone calls, and expresses love for the congregation. If people have great respect for the work of the pastor, they will not be concerned about the pastor's usage of time.

If a pastor's responsibilities have him or her working late at night and into the morning hours, then sleeping until mid-morning, that may be difficult for some laity to handle. Many people identify late rising with laziness, even if the person only gets seven or eight hours of sleep. How can a pastor with this schedule please his or her people? Can the pastor make it known what he or she is doing until one or two o'clock in the morning? If it is spent working on sermons, catching up on professional reading, or preparing material for teaching, people will understand that. If it is watching movies or playing games on the Internet, then convincing the laity that this is a faithful use of time is going to be more of a challenge. Trying to convince God that this is a legitimate use of time may be the bigger issue. If a church is healthy and is filled with joy, inspired worship, and a strong mission program, the laity will not care much about the pastor's sleeping habits.

God Can Use Schedules

We hit where we aim. When we create schedules for our work, God will honor that and will usually help us meet our schedules. An unscheduled life is usually a less goal-oriented life. By following a weekly schedule for work, we can become more productive and achieve our goals. The unscheduled life that is less intentional is usually less fruitful.

Time management is not the same as keeping busy. All of us are super busy. There is a vast difference between time management and busyness. We are going to be busy whether we manage our time or not. Managing our time makes more sense of our busy-ness. It helps us to have more control, and it gives us power to take stress out of our time constraints. You are more loving to yourself and to God when you manage your time conscientiously, rather than letting time push you around.

My friend Jim was a top businessman in Chicago, running a company with two thousand employees. He was known in Chicago not only for his business acumen but also for his community involvement. As CEO of this large company, Jim had access to money, so he hired a time management consultant to follow him around for two to three days to help him know how to manage his time better.

After Jim retired, I asked him if he would come to Friendship Church in Bolingbrook, Illinois, to teach a course on effective time management. He agreed, and we met from 8:30 until 11:30 on four Saturday mornings. It was enormously helpful to our laypeople and to me. You may have businesspeople in your church who understand time management. Ask them to conduct a four-week series for your church members. Your church will be blessed.

Our Time Is God's Time

Time is life, and thus, it belongs to God. How we use our time will determine how we honor God. Paul wrote to the Ephesians, "Be careful then how you live, not as unwise people but as wise, making the most of the time, because the days are evil" (Eph 5:15-16).

Again, he wrote to the Christians in Colossae, "Conduct yourselves wisely toward outsiders, making the most of the time" (4:5). Jesus said, "From everyone to whom much has been given, much will be required;

and from the one to whom much has been entrusted, even more will be demanded" (Luke 12:48). God gives us each enough time to complete whatever tasks lie before us. We are told to use our time wisely, in order to finish the things of most importance. When that happens, God will be pleased with our lives.

Because we often feel torn in trying to finish many jobs, time management does not add to our stress, but, indeed, takes it away. Let me give you an illustration. I was at the church in the afternoon and evening during my ministry. However, I used to block out time on my weekly calendar from four-thirty until six-thirty, Monday through Thursday evenings, because that was time for Rita. My marriage was so important that I scheduled time for it. Also, Friday night was date night for Rita and me. It had to be a very, very unusual event that interfered with that wonderful night out.

A schedule helps guard you, so you have more control of your life. If you have a son playing a ball game or a daughter who is playing in a concert, you can tell people that you have an appointment and that you are not available for anything else.

We Methodists are here today because our Wesleyan ancestors felt the importance of correctly using their time. Why are we asked to promise at our ordination that we will not spend any more time in one place than is necessary? We are asked, because the organizational genius, John Wesley, lived that way himself, and he expected proper time management from the people who worked in his organization.

Prioritizing Is the Key Issue

The Scriptures encourage us to bring our first fruits to God because if we don't pay our tithe up front, we will find all kinds of other ways to spend that money. Prioritizing our time is the same. It means doing the important things first. If we don't do the important stuff first, it will not get done. We will find other ways to spend our time.

You can illustrate this principle for your people in a sermon, Sunday school class, or youth meeting. Use golf balls for the important things in life and sand for the less significant. First, fill a quart jar with golf balls, and then add sand until the jar is full. Now reverse the process, and put the sand into the jar first. When you try to add the golf balls, you will not be able to get as many golf balls into the jar as before.

By filling our lives with little stuff first, we have less time to get the big things done. But if we put first things first, we still have time for other things.

We are all the same. What are we likely to do first? It will probably be the stuff we are best at doing or the stuff we like to do the most; it usually means we do the easiest stuff first. It takes a lot of discipline to do the most important work first. The demon of laziness tugs at the heart of everyone.

What is the most important thing for you to be doing each week? What is your number one task? What task can God use, more than any other, to bring people to Christ and to the church? If worship is the central activity of the congregation each week, and the sermon is the most important part of worship, then preparing the sermon ought to get priority in scheduling. I once had dinner with a well-known author. He had written many books and I asked when he did his writing. He said he wrote from six o'clock until ten o'clock every morning. He put first things first, and his discipline bore great fruit.

Naturally, our vision for Christ, our passion to bring people to the Savior, ought to be number one. But, then, how do we put bones together for a skeleton in order to flesh that out? What is involved in living out your vision and your passion? What kind of schedule can help you do that?

Can one be too schedule bound? One of the weaknesses of having a rigid schedule is that I feel I have sometimes scheduled the Holy Spirit out of my life. I was so tight in my scheduling that when an opportunity to witness or to make a contact came up, I had something else scheduled. However, my guess is that the times I have been true to Jesus Christ far outnumber and outweigh the few times when I have missed an opportunity because of my rigid schedule.

I challenge you to think through and plan every week as to how you will spend your time. If you have not done this, try it, as it will change your life. It will organize everything better for you so you will likely feel less stress. Also, it will help you to prioritize things so you will get the most important things done. Prayerfully, that will allow God to use your life most effectively so you can succeed at making more disciples of Jesus Christ. If all of these things happen, then you will also be a happier and more peaceful person. Finally, when you come to the end of your career, you will be able to look back and say that you did the best you could do.

If you don't already schedule your days, it is not going to be easy for you to change; but God is able to help you. Pray about this, asking Jesus to help you manage your time most effectively; and because he cares so much for you, he will help you.

Discussion questions

1. How do you plan your weekly schedule now?
2. If you feel Jesus Christ would be honored more by your creating a weekly schedule, how will you accomplish that?
3. What needs to be given more priority in your life?
4. What are you willing to do to make positive changes?
5. What do you need to learn to say "no" to?
6. How can you get the help you need to learn to manage your time better?
7. What businessperson can you invite to teach an effective time management seminar in your church?

Note

1. Advertisement for *Time Challenged*, a Video or DVD program, http://www.business-marketing.com/store/stressmanagement.html (accessed August 30, 2006).

2. Stephen R. Covey, A. Roger Merrill, and Rebecca R. Merrill, *First Things First* (New York: Simon and Schuster, 1994), 155.

9

Leadership Recruitment: Getting More Done Without Working Harder

vangelism in the small membership church happens most effectively when a large percentage of the congregation is involved in
the work of Christ. Furthermore, it is exciting to see people grow
by giving of themselves. Early in my ministry I felt reluctant to give people tasks to complete, because I felt I was infringing on their time. I
learned later that God blesses people as they become involved in ministry. Yes, it obviously takes time, but it is life-giving. By recruiting people for ministry, I realized I was letting God bring them new and deeper
life instead of imposing on them.

Indeed, serving Jesus Christ is our salvation. Jesus said, "Those who
find their life will lose it, and those who lose their life for my sake will find
it" (Matt 10:39). That has become one of the most meaningful verses in
the Bible for me. We grow and find fulfillment in life when we give ourselves in service for Jesus Christ. It brings excitement into a boring life.
Serving Jesus Christ transforms a frustrated life into one of meaning.

How Can the Pastor Multiply Himself or Herself?

Not only does involving people in ministry help them grow but it
also multiplies the life of the pastor. The pastor's time and energy are

limited, so God needs others to do the work of God. By involving others, God is able to accomplish much more work for the kingdom.

Effective pastors recruit and develop good leadership that multiplies ministries. Pastor, your ability to recruit and develop leadership is going to determine the effectiveness of your ministry. God will accomplish more through you, and you will find more excitement as you encourage more people to be involved in ministry.

Trust and Respect Develop Effective Leadership Teams

Hardworking pastors win the trust and respect of their laity. Someone extolled the respect a football coach had from his players. He said that the players held the coach in such high esteem that they would run through a wall for him. Hardworking, upright, and loving pastors win such respect that laity will go to great lengths to serve Christ for him or her. They will volunteer many hours of work; they will do unexpected things; and they will step forward with courage and dedication during the cold of winter and the heat of summer. Someone has said, "Anyone who thinks they are leading and has no one behind them is only taking a walk."

Trust is utterly important for building leadership teams. I always considered the members of my congregations my friends. I have heard clergy talk about getting away from their churches so they could let their hair down. I never understood that, because I felt I could have fun with my laity. We had a blast when we met with our Young Couples Club for their potluck dinner, followed by games. Playing volleyball on game night was always a lot of fun, and going on family hayrides on lovely October evenings was always so enjoyable. My wife and I always had a ball with our 45-Plus Couples Club as we played hilarious games or went to plays or ballgames together.

I mention these things because I think that these kinds of close relationships are related to building effective leadership teams. They are important because when people see us playing and laughing with them it builds a close bond. They know they can trust us.

Mack is a wonderful, crusty Texan, who has literally traveled the world with his lovely wife, Doris. They came to Friendship Church in Bolingbrook, Illinois, in 1989. Although people of faith, they had never really been active in a church before. Mack and Doris accepted the love we gave them, and they poured themselves into that church. Mack had been trained in air-conditioning years earlier, so he installed our first air-conditioning system in the church—didn't charge us a penny for it, and worked in some of the hottest and most uncomfortable conditions doing it. Our worship attendance went up 26 percent the first summer we had air-conditioning. Mack and Doris became friends of many in the congregation, and as their children were grown like ours, we developed a special bond and had many Sunday noon dinners together in a vast array of Chicago suburban restaurants. Mack's self-giving was due to the loving relationships and trust he and Doris developed with the church.

Mack retired about 1996 and they moved back to Texas. I was deeply touched when they said, time and again, that those seven years at Friendship Church were the best years of their lives. Even though their children and grandchildren all lived in Texas, they considered moving back to Bolingbrook, Illinois, because of their church experience. Their joyous relationships, deep involvement, and self-giving were so memorable to them.

Effective pastors are able to develop leadership teams that will make enormous sacrifices for the work of Jesus Christ. Paid and unpaid staff will go out in rain or snow, hot or cold, and put in untold hours, because they feel so good about serving Jesus Christ. Ideally, we would like to say that they should do it only for Christ, and they should. However, they are also motivated because the pastor and pastoral team are the ambassadors of Jesus Christ to them. They are touched and motivated by Jesus through the leaders that Jesus has given them.

Developing effective leadership teams involves respect. When laity see their clergy lay down their lives serving others, they develop an emulating respect. They see their leader willing to lead the charge, so they are willing to follow.

We can talk about every recruiting principle that is available to build church leadership, but it will be to no avail if the clergy are not trusted or respected by their laypeople. Deep trust and high respect are fundamental to building strong leadership teams.

Ministries of a Paid Staff

Every church needs a strong paid staff in order to move ahead. Whether you have a church of one hundred at worship or twenty-five, you need paid staff in addition to yourself. The growth and health of your church will depend upon your paid staff. When I arrived at Friendship Church we had paid staff of five. When I retired, I was managing a staff of twenty. When I arrived, they had an organist, choir director, janitorial service, secretary, and me. The first positions we added were a part-time Director of Christian Education and a part-time Youth Director.

Along the way we added a preschool program that involved three staff positions and a Parents' Day Out that had three on staff. These two programs were helpful in fulfilling our mission of making disciples of Jesus Christ, because they allowed Christian ministry to children and also brought new members to the church. These two programs also brought in enough money to help fund another part-time position for the church. Another $8000 of income allows you to pay someone ten dollars an hour for fifteen hours a week, working in some area that will help your church. Gradually, we added these other part-time positions: Director of Singles Ministry, Director of Evangelism, Volunteer coordinator, Music coordinator, Director of Contemporary Music, Visitation minister, and two full-time secretaries.

I adopted the model advocated by Lyle Schaller of using part-time lay staff. Each local church has enormously gifted laypeople who are willing to work for reasonable salaries. Plus, they are highly committed because they are working for their church. They feel honored that their church asked them to work for the congregation.

The upside to this part-time model is that you get a whole lot more done for less money. When you add an ordained pastor, you will likely spend around $60,000 a year, when you add pension and insurance money. For that amount of money, by using the part-time lay model, you can add three or four people, who will likely accomplish more than the one pastor would. Plus, there is the richness of multiple personalities, which can attract a variety of people. Someone may say that it is taking advantage of people not to pay their health insurance, but my answer is that a lot of people in your churches have insurance coverage through their spouses.

Some people feel that it is too risky to hire from within your church, but I have found the opposite to be true. It hurt us once or twice in the fourteen-plus years, but I am not sure it would have made much difference if the people had been non-members.

The downside of the part-time lay staff model is the difficulty of supervision. It is very time-consuming to supervise a staff of twenty. How did we do it? Naturally, we had our weekly staff meetings and our annual fall retreat. Plus, I tried to schedule time to meet with each one, but I didn't handle that well. I made sure each one felt that I had an open door for them, so they could come to talk any time they wished. We made sure the staff always received a very nice Christmas gift and a nice Christmas party. Plus, the Staff Parish Relations committee divided the staff among the committee members and took responsibility to keep in touch with them to make sure they were happy.

Also, every time I saw the staff working, I thanked them. The two most important words of supervision are, "Thank you." Both paid staff and volunteers appreciate those two words. I spent a lot of time saying thank you, and I was sincere in saying it. It is an honor to have people pour out their lives for ministry, which is a direct gift to you. Money isn't enough to keep people working for you, but a happy environment where they feel appreciated and are free to do their work is. Just a word about what you name your staff positions. We used to call Pat our janitor, but then I felt it would be so much more dignified to call her our Building Manager. She, in fact, spent a lot of time assigning activities to different rooms. We were bulging at the seams with night and weekend activities, so it was hard to find space for everyone. But I am sure that Pat felt so much better being our Building Manager rather than our janitor or custodian. Also, I renamed and redefined our secretary's position to become our Administrative Assistant, which she truly was. She took many loads off my shoulders administratively, and she felt more dignified in being my Administrative Assistant.

It is very important that you have enough paid staff to handle the workload. Adding staff is not as hard as churches think it is. If your mortgage is soon to be paid off, what are you going to do with the extra money? Use it to hire another staff person.

If you have developed trust and respect from your laity, they want two things to happen. First, many want their church to grow, so they will likely be persuaded that you should add paid staff. Second, they do not want to see their pastor burned out. People told me that they were worried that I was putting in too many hours. When they talk like that, they are willing to pay additional staff.

How to Enlarge Your Paid Staff

Some will ask why it is necessary to pay someone to take a certain job. They want to know why a volunteer can't fill that position.

Churches pay people for at least three reasons. First, there are the skilled positions. For example, it would be hard to find a volunteer in the church to play an instrument, direct a choir, or lead a contemporary orchestra so well that God will attract many to come to worship because of the music leadership. Therefore, you pay for skilled positions. Second, you pay for positions that are so important they are considered essential, and it will help the church enormously if programs in these areas are fully developed. Education and youth are perhaps the two most important areas in this regard. Third, churches pay because some positions take a lot of time; it is unfair and unrealistic to expect anybody to volunteer for them. We were committed to contemporary music in worship, and even though we had guitarists and drummers in the congregation, it took time to coordinate their efforts. It was unrealistic for anyone to give all that time without remuneration.

Do all that you can in order to enlarge your paid staff. For example, every church should at least have a secretary. There is no excuse for a pastor to have to type the weekly bulletin. If you are a pastor, it is too expensive for the church to be paying you to do the secretarial work, plus it is taking away from your primary work. You should be doing the work that only you can do.

Wherever possible add paid staff. Pick the right people, and God will help your church grow. Multiply yourself by giving God more arms, legs, voices, and energies to bring people to Christ through your church. You deserve all the help you can get in order to build your church.

Building the Volunteer Staff

The health of your church is determined by the involvement of your laity. The laypersons or unpaid retired clergy in your congregation are your volunteer staff. These are the folks who put their shoulders to the wheel to build the kingdom through your church. Obviously, if anything significant is going to happen in your church, you need laypeople working with you. The laity make up the church, and laity make the church move. If any growth is going to come to your congregation, the laypeople will generate it, nurture it, and sustain it.

Every church has laity sitting on the sidelines. You have many who are uninvolved. A large percentage of them will be pleased to get involved in the right group, task, or role. They all feel better when they are making a contribution to the kingdom of God. If they can help make a difference, they get excited about it.

There are two principal ways to get laity involved. The first is to announce something in the bulletin or newsletter, inviting people to sign up. These are the general jobs, which anybody can perform, such as ushering, mowing grass, a spring cleanup around the churchyard, and so forth. Much of the work in the church fits under this category. Ask people to write their names on a piece of paper in the bulletin and drop the paper in the offering plate as it passes. Don't put the sign-up list in the hall somewhere, so the people have to remember to sign it after the service. Make it as easy as possible. They respond most readily with the fewest hoops to jump through.

Then there are the more specialized jobs. Being treasurer of the church is perhaps the most important. You never want to invite just anyone to be your treasurer. You want your best people, who know money, who know the computer, and who are very disciplined to be your treasurer. Here is where the Lay Leadership Committee is very useful. I visited a church recently where they announced in worship that they needed someone to volunteer to be treasurer. I would never have done that. I wanted someone who knew the computer, and could produce a treasurer's report for me at the end of the month.

When my nominating committee (as we called it then) met, we coded the entire church membership role, indicating the involvement of each member. As we went through the list, we knew who served in a task or role, or who was in a group. We tried to get everyone involved. When the bulletin said that every member of the church was a minister, we wanted that to be real. Everyone was to be serving or involved in some capacity.

Trust Is a Two-Way Street

If you are a pastor, do you trust your laity to have authority to help you run the church? Effective pastors are secure enough to allow laity to share leadership. Seventy-five people were trained as Stephen Ministers through Friendship Church, and I met monthly with the leaders to discuss how people were ministering. Often I knew of people who could use a Stephen Minister, and I brought those names to the meeting. One reason we had a phenomenal Stephen Ministry program is because the laity were trusted. We were thankful for them, as they were willing to minister to needy and troubled people in the church and the community. By trusting our Stephen Ministers, God multiplied my ministry many times over. God was ministering to people for many hours each month through the laity, which I could never have done alone.

Our Stephen Ministry leaders often returned from area meetings where Stephen Ministers from other churches reported that they were not assigned persons to minister to. Their Stephen Ministry work was inactive, because their pastors did not trust the laity to be ministering to hurting people in the congregation. For some strange reason the pastor felt threatened to share his or her ministry. Many Stephen Ministry programs become stifled for that reason.

Effective pastors constantly bring in fresh leadership whenever possible. Two of every five leaders in your church should have joined the church within the last five years. Also, growing churches have many leaders between the ages of twenty-five and forty. New members bring fresh ideas and new energy to a church.

Pastors, you should only do the things that no one else can do. Everybody can cut the grass, or paint and clean the church, but nobody else can make contacts for the church like you can. Visiting the unchurched and participating where the unchurched can be reached is the pastor's job. Making disciples of Jesus Christ is central to the pastor's job. But in order to do that, the pastor has to have built teams to attend to other very important work. The laity often complete these tasks better than the pastor and are fulfilled in having a part in ministry.

God Builds Healthy Churches through Team Leadership

Effective churches operate out of a form of team leadership. The first Biblical example of that is Moses and his father-in-law, Jethro. Jethro came to visit Moses and saw how he was surrounded by people every day coming for counsel. Hundreds of people were waiting to see Moses to ask for his help. Every day was the same without any letup. "Moses' father-in-law said to him, 'What you are doing is not good. You will surely wear yourself out, both you and these people with you. For the task is too heavy for you; you cannot do it alone'" (Exod 18:17-18). Pastors who try to do it all will also suffer burnout. So the wise father-in-law said to Moses, "You should also look for able men among all the people, men who fear God, are trustworthy, and hate dishonest gain; set such men over them as officers over thousands, hundreds, fifties, and tens" (Exod 18:21). One person at the top oversees ten, those ten oversee fifty, those fifty oversee several hundred and those several hundred oversee thousands. This is pyramid leadership. The church was begun with Jesus choosing twelve disciples to begin the work, and those twelve recruited others.

Effective pastors are always building teams. This is a learned process. When I was working on my doctorate, Professor Rogers of Northwestern University who was on my congregational supervisory group, said to me, "Royal, do you always want to be in the trenches?" He saw that I wasn't recruiting people to do things but was always trying to do them myself. Early in my ministry I rode the lawn mower at the church. During my last years I didn't even want to know how to start the lawn mower. Teams of six to eight men and older youth mowed the grass from April to October.

Greasing the Leadership Machinery

How do you keep the leadership team happy and functioning well? One basic way is to show genuine appreciation. When people serve, they appreciate a simple word of affirmation, and it is so easy to give. When I saw people mowing our huge lawn, I would often interrupt what I was doing just to walk outside to say, "Thank you." Words of thanks should be freely shared with both paid and unpaid staff. We all enjoy hearing the words, "Thank you."

Qualities of True Leaders

Effective leaders are servant leaders. They lay down their lives as Jesus laid down his life. They are sacrificial givers. They are tithers or are moving toward the tithe. A church is not wise to put people into leadership positions who are not committed to Jesus Christ with their giving. Money is an important part of our lives, and if God is not Lord of our checkbooks, then a huge portion of our lives remains uncommitted to God. Effective churches have model leaders in their financial giving.

We need leaders in the church who are fully committed to Jesus in all of life, including their financial giving.

Effective church leaders are committed to servant leadership. They are not self-centered or self-serving. I hope that as a leader, you will pray the prayer that I still pray very often, "Lord, please help me to be humble. Don't let me think more highly of myself than I ought to think."

Effective leaders stay focused on the big picture. They will not be distracted from the real purpose of the church. They are willing to pay a price to get the job done. They are so focused that they have little time for small thinking, and they do not get involved in pettiness. Effective leaders are willing to give up personal agendas. They adopt a servant leadership. They are serving to please Jesus Christ and not themselves. Effective leaders pay attention to progress. They want good church records, so they can see how the church is progressing.

Effective church leaders take a positive approach to life and are honest about the church's current situation. They do not want to be involved in playing games, so they are not in denial. They want reality and truth. However, they try to solve negative situations in a positive way. They don't say, "Things are going bad." Rather, they ask, "How can we fix this?" And through it all they stay spiritually healthy.

Effective leaders don't want everything their way. A pastor told his church that he saw a need for a new lawn sign for their very busy highway. One of the parishioners said, "If they get the sign, I am quitting the church." God can't get anything done in a church with such petty thinking.

Effective leaders strive to be spiritually healthy. They read God's word so they can walk with God daily. They read it so they can be inspired to be more than they could otherwise be. They stay in touch with Jesus Christ through daily prayer. They commit themselves to spiritual disciplines. They are in worship unless they are sick or out of town. When they are out of town, they worship elsewhere, because they want to stay in close touch with God. They have a personal devotional life alone, or with the family at home, or in their office at work. They participate in Sunday school, Bible Study, or a small group. They begin meetings with prayer.

God Needs Clergy and Lay Teams

I have heard clergy complain about laity over the years, and I have said to them, "I feel sorry for the laity, because they often have to sit and watch a revolving door of pastors." On the other hand, laypeople often don't know how difficult it is to run a church. Pastoring a church is a complicated task.

In order for God to create a healthy growing church, the pastor has to develop a vision with the laity. That requires openness and patience on the part of the laity. Many laity also have a vision for their church. It is important that those visions overlap. Through prayer and communication, healthy churches have clergy and laity with a common vision in order to make disciples of Jesus Christ.

In churches that are alive and growing the pastors and laity are a team, and they work to have a common vision. The pastor has to have ultimate authority, but that authority is used to create teams of workers for Jesus Christ. The only power of the church is the power of the Holy Spirit. This kind of leadership team is always spiritually grounded in Jesus Christ. It remains open to God's emerging vision, and that leads to the church's finest day. This leadership team concept is just as important for the small membership church as it is for the large membership church.

Discussion questions

1. Who are the most involved people of our church? What percentage of the total membership are they? How can we get more of our people involved in Christ's work in our church?
2. How can we make our leadership team more effective?
3. Are we getting the best people into the most important jobs? Do we have obstacles to recruiting leaders?
4. Are we doing everything we can in training our leaders? What kinds of training do I need?
5. Is there a way that we can increase our paid staff? If so, what would be the staff position(s), and what do I need to do to make it happen?
6. How can we improve the recruitment of volunteers in our church? Do we want to make this improvement?

10

Choices: Offer Them and They Will Come

Small membership churches can think and act big. Often small membership church leaders do not see possibilities that are very real for them. When considering options, I encourage you, as a small membership church leader, to think about providing your members and prospective members with the richest Christian experiences possible.

People want options, and if you offer them options, they will come. What is the most popular convenience store in your community? What is the biggest grocery store chain? Which of these has the largest parking lot? The chain grocery store does. Why? What is the reason the big store needs the bigger parking lot? The answer is that it offers many more options than the convenience store. How many kinds of cereal can you buy at the convenience store? Perhaps only four, such as one brand each of wheat, oats, corn, and rice, and a couple of these may be heavily sugared. How many kinds of cereal can you buy at the chain store? Your choices include: a whole aisle full with perhaps seventy brands including hot or cold cereals, plain cornflakes, or five different kinds of multi-grain cereals. You can even buy cereal with blueberries, raisins, or pecans.

People go in larger numbers to places that provide them with more options. That is true of a twelve-screen theater in comparison to the little one-screen theater in the neighborhood. It is true of furniture and appliance stores. And, it is also true of the church. People attend the churches in greatest number that provide them with the most options.

Offering Worship Options

Many churches would increase their weekly worship attendance if they added another worship service. Friendship Church had two Christmas Eve Services, averaging about 500 in 1987. We added a third service, and our numbers went up. Then we added a fourth service, so we offered them at five, seven, nine, and eleven o'clock; and our numbers climbed to 800. Why? Because some people wanted to bring their children to the children's service at five o'clock, where we made noise, ringing bells. Others wanted to hear the contemporary instruments used in our Christmas Eve singing at seven o'clock, while others preferred to come at nine o'clock. Then there were those for whom the eleven o'clock service was more precious. They wanted to hear the chancel choir. We gave options for different times plus different service styles. Many chose their worship service simply because of the hour it was being offered.

We did the same thing on Easter morning. We had three services: six-thirty, nine o'clock, and ten-thirty. Then we inserted a fourth service, changing the times to six-thirty, eight o'clock, nine-thirty, and eleven o'clock. Worship attendance increased from about 500 to 600 by adding another time option. Instead of taking away from the other services, it attracted new people. If you offer options, the people will come.

Saturday evening services are common across America today. Usually they begin small but may grow to thirty or forty. During the early stages of growth, people may ask, "Is this worth it, just for thirty to forty people?" If this is your church's situation, you can answer that in three ways. Your total church attendance for the weekend would drop without that Saturday service. Whenever you eliminate options the church loses. Second, there are tens of thousands of churches across America that don't average more than thirty in worship for the whole weekend. Third, it is a loving act to give people options, whenever possible.

Why do people attend Saturday evening services? Some simply prefer to worship on Saturday evening. Then there are Sunday morning people who have a Sunday morning conflict, but they still want to worship. They are thankful they can worship on Saturday evening. Then there are people who work on Sundays who are grateful for a Saturday service. Otherwise, they could not worship regularly without going to a different church. Also, it gives visitors another option and opportunity to check out your church.

No church is too small to offer worship options. Leith Anderson tells of Westminster Presbyterian Church in Duluth, Minnesota. It was averaging forty in worship in 1995, and had plateaued at that number for many years. They added a second Sunday morning service, but not because they were crowded, either in the sanctuary or in the parking lot. They just wanted to give their members and visitors another worship option on Sunday morning. Two years later their average Sunday morning attendance was more than 200. God used a second option to help them grow. People want options, and when you give them, they will come.[1]

People Want Discipleship Options

People want study opportunities that fit their interests. Some prefer Sunday school classes, while others want a weeknight class. Home study groups do very well, while other groups feel most comfortable meeting in the church. People are attracted to Bible studies, theological discussions, and classes on social issues. Many are in need of practical groups dealing with marriage, parenting, depression, or cancer.

I insisted on having two options for vacation Bible schools. In our community many families vacationed right after school in June and missed the June VBS. So we offered another the first week in August, when kids were already bored yet had two weeks before the beginning of school. So what if some kids came to both sessions of the vacation Bible school. It takes a lot of work, but how much do we care about children? Does it matter if children believe in Jesus Christ? The answer to that question may spur us on to offer more options for them.

Movies provide opportunities not only for fellowship and entertainment but also for spiritual growth. Countless churches across America rode the publicity wave and offered their people an opportunity to go to see the *Passion of the Christ* together. They followed the movie with discussion groups, where many learned anew about the life and death of Jesus. One church rented a theater to have worship around a showing of the *End of the Spear*. That was also true of *The Lion, the Witch, and the Wardrobe*.

Book studies are available for your people on virtually any subject. Many churches provided a group to study together Rick Warren's *Purpose Driven Life*. Your people know about this book through the secular press, as it was on the *New York Times* best-seller list. Incredibly, more than 26 million copies have been sold.

How we spend our money is certainly a spiritual matter. Do people struggling with finances have an option to receive help in your church? Do you have a financial consultant in your church who would be glad to conduct a Saturday morning seminar to help people think through budgeting, investing, saving, the wise use of credit cards, and paying off debts? A church in Illinois with about one hundred in average worship attendance offered a study on money management. Twenty-six people attended for several weeks. Many were people from outside the church.

Fellowship Options Are Important

The health quotient of a church is determined by how much time members of a church spend with each other outside of the church building during the week. Members of healthy churches get to know each other and enjoy time together beyond church activities. Families gather for cookouts and picnics. Singles find strength in fellowship with each other. The church can enhance these relationships by offering options in social programs.

The vast majority of churches have sports lovers who enjoy playing various games. Some would find much joy in a golf league. Others enjoy bowling, while softball is a favorite to some. Still others find their fulfillment through volleyball or basketball. Small membership churches are able to offer such fun options to their people. School officials are very happy to allow churches to rent their facilities for a reasonable amount for these events.

Attending athletic events is a way of helping church members enjoy time together. Both the young, who are able to play sports, as well as those who are past their playing days, enjoy watching games. They enjoy all levels of sports, be they high school, college, semi-professional, or professional. We used to rent a bus to drive into Chicago to watch the Chicago Bulls.

Virtually all churches have many senior citizens, and offering a senior fellowship option can be very easy. I sat beside a senior from a Lutheran church many years ago who told me about their monthly senior luncheon. After the church provided a meal, the members either attended a program or played a game. We adopted that idea, and it worked beautifully. Younger families volunteered to provide the food, and they considered it a joy. Smiles and laughter filled the room as the seniors enjoyed fellowship with each other, and new people were being reached.

Options to Create Healthy Families

Sanctification is a basic Christian doctrine that touches every aspect of daily life. Christ needs to be involved in our play and our personal relationships. Jesus wants to be part of marriages and parenting. What options can we offer people?

Newspapers often list pages of support groups offering help for virtually every human need. The church can offer healing and support groups that have a Christian base. Often Christian counselors in a community are available to guide such groups in small churches. Their fees are often reasonable, and they can provide help that the pastor is neither skilled to give or is too busy to offer.

Naturally, what you offer needs to be well done. Not everything costs an arm and a leg, and often people are willing to pay for something if it is really important to them. You have many people in your churches and communities who would be glad to give of themselves. They simply need to be asked.

Offering Service Options

Faithful disciples of Jesus Christ want to give of themselves in service to God. Options are also important in terms of how we help our people become involved. Offering your people a list with a variety of ministerial opportunities ignites interest in serving Jesus Christ, not only in your faithful members but also in visitors. Sincere disciples want to serve Jesus Christ, but they desire places that fit their gifts. Some may know their spiritual gifts and are looking for options to give of themselves. However, they may be reluctant to get involved until they see something that really excites them.

Rural or small-town churches may create much excitement by taking a turn at providing food for a homeless shelter in a nearby city. Many small membership churches in the suburbs or city provide their members much satisfaction by taking a turn at giving overnight shelter to the homeless through a local organization. I have personally experienced the joy of working with the homeless and have seen that same joy in the eyes of countless laity.

Adults and youth get excited about taking a mission trip to Appalachia, an inner city area, an Indian reservation, or some other place of need in the states. Some churches stretch themselves by taking mission groups to other countries where there is enormous need.

Hurricane Katrina created such devastation that there will be needs in Louisiana and Mississippi for many years. Both laity and clergy find great fulfillment in serving Jesus Christ to help those in continued need.

Habitat for Humanity chapters are found across the nation. They are open to a few people from a small membership church, coming to help build homes for the needy.

If people sign up to serve or make it audibly known, then it is utterly important to provide them the opportunity. Laity become discouraged when they have volunteered for work in the church, but no one calls to accept their offer. A church run with integrity will do everything possible to follow through with persons wishing to participate in the life of the church.

Discussion questions

1. What new options can we offer our people?
2. How can we find out what options our people would like?
3. What needs exist in our community or the world that Jesus Christ is calling us to help fill?
4. How and when will we decide to let God meet these needs of the community through us?
5. What resources exist in our community that would help us offer more options?

Note

1. Leith Anderson, *Leadership That Works* (Minneapolis: Bethany House, 1999), 87.

11

Hospitality: Outdoing Wal-Mart in Welcoming People to Your Church

It is not easy for unchurched people to visit a church. The churched find it very easy to walk through the doors of their home church. However, the churched looking for a new church home may have anxiety entering a new congregation. The unchurched likely find it difficult entering *any* church, not knowing what to expect amidst strangers in a meeting they know nothing about. That can be a very frightening experience. I remember one visitor told me that she sat in our parking lot for twenty-five minutes before she got courage to leave her car and walk into the building.

It is very important to make both our members and visitors feel most welcome in our churches. There are ways to make visitors feel wanted, valued, and accepted. We can create such a wonderful atmosphere in our churches that people will want to come back.

If the church is serious about reaching people and making disciples of Jesus Christ, it has to be ready for company. We need to give careful attention to what happens to first-time visitors from the moment they enter our parking lot to the minute they exit.

Welcoming Begins in the Parking Lot

Whether a church has a parking problem or not, people feel welcomed when they see a parking lot attendant. A friendly person welcoming people even before they enter the church building is very impressive to visitors and enjoyable for members.

If the church has a parking problem, then the attendant becomes an usher, helping people to find the most convenient parking spot. On rainy days, the attendant can help elderly people into the church with an umbrella. Depending on the size of the small congregation, having parking lot attendants gives the church another place for people to get involved.

Two or more parking spaces marked with visitor signs immediately help visitors know that they are important. Those welcoming symbols make a very positive first impression. Newcomers know you care for them.

Churches in snow country will make worship easier for members and impress visitors if they get their parking lots cleared of snow. Living in Illinois, I experienced two different church parking lots on consecutive snowy Sundays. One lot had four inches of snow, and the other was plowed clean. Any visitor looking for a church home would have been impressed with the one church and unimpressed with the other, partly because of the parking lot. If everything else were equal, the respective parking lots would have been the deciding factor in which church they chose.

It is obvious to all that well-kept church grounds with manicured lawns and lovely flower beds smile a welcoming feeling to people.

Does Your Outside Sign Bring Visitors Inside?

Church lawn signs are used by God to help churches grow. Visitors often enter churches because of lawn signs. If you have a lawn sign, how many people read it? The answer is dependent on whether it is parallel or perpendicular to your church. About 80 percent of drivers read a lawn sign that is perpendicular to the street, while about 20 percent read one that is parallel to the street. Unless a sign stares people in the face, most are not curious enough to turn their heads to see what a sign says.

If people do look at it, can they read it? Signs with letters smaller than five inches are illegible. Large letters that are well spaced make for readable signs. Too much clutter makes a sign more difficult to read and less attractive, so it takes away some of the punch.

What do you have on your sign? Unless sermon titles are really catchy, how many people come to visit a church because of sermon titles? A church that has clever sayings mixed with humor and pithy meaning can get the attention of drivers. Visitors to our worship services often mentioned our lawn sign as a reason they became motivated to worship with us.

How often is it changed? In order for well-placed, attractive, well-lighted lawn signs with interesting messages to bring in new people, they have to be kept up-to-date. Passersby will stop looking at a sign if it has the same message week after week. Changing a sign twice a week keeps fresh words for the public, which also tells them this church is organized. Indeed, it takes organization, but that is another gift to the church. It provides more opportunities for people to serve.

Smiling Greeters and Helpful Ushers

If you are trying to attract and keep younger people in your church, what age group of greeters and ushers will most likely make that happen? Obviously, young- and middle-aged people are attracted by people their age. Older people are generally very gracious and do a great job of greeting and ushering, but the wise church intentionally adds younger people to those jobs.

Finding smiling, pleasant greeters, and effectively training ushers takes a lot of time and effort. Greeters and ushers should know where the nursery and Sunday school rooms are and what kind of Sunday school classes the church has. Having written guidelines for the ushers and greeters, along with regular training sessions, allows God to make people feel more at home in a church.

Making Your Building Say "Welcome"

New church buildings always attract more people, because people want to associate with what is new. This is also true in the business world, as people flock to new restaurant and store buildings. New buildings with fresh paint and new carpet have a very welcoming atmosphere.

Old buildings can also say welcome. Does the place look bright or dingy? Is the building free from junk? Lovely entryways, nicely painted and decorated walls, well-kept carpets or flooring, and brightly lighted halls and sanctuary in any church building will help people feel comfortable. Bathrooms are more important than most church people realize. Bowls of potpourri in both bathrooms, along with flowers and female items, including lotion, in the women's bathroom, will impress visitors and bring them back. A small membership church with a new building will be wise to include a baby changing area along with materials.

What about signage inside? Are there clear and obvious signs to washrooms, Sunday school rooms, and the fellowship area? Are the coat racks easily accessible and spacious, with solid, attractive hangers for coats?

Getting Info on Your Visitors without Seeming Snoopy

Do you attempt to contact the visitors who attended your worship services? You can only contact them if you know who they are. How do you learn their names, addresses, and telephone numbers?

The best way to get that information is through the use of a fellowship pad. Everybody in the pew is inclined to sign a pad coming down the row. Psychologically, people are more apt to do what the person next to them did. The fellowship pad is likely to get more information than having a slip of paper in the bulletin for people to sign and place in the offering plate. People easily ignore a slip of paper but feel compelled to sign a pad coming down the aisle. However, the fellowship pad has to include a sharpened pencil for people to use.

The importance of the fellowship pad is stressed when it is passed out during the service instead of lying in the pew when the service begins. As the ushers pass out the pads during the service, it obviously draws attention to the pad and makes it apparent to everybody that this is something of importance.

What can you say that will make both members and visitors more likely to sign the pads? Telling people, "We want you to register your attendance today," or, "At this time we would like to have you sign the registration pad," gives members and visitors a sense that they are in school or at an organizational meeting. Generally, visitors will feel less threatened and inhibited if they hear words like, "Please sign the fellowship pad as it comes down your row, as it will help us in our ministry." That language may make visitors feel less like they are making a commitment to the church and more like they are actually helping the church. There is a huge difference.

How to Recognize Visitors Without Embarrassing Them

America has changed over the last forty years to a more anonymous society. This may be particularly true in the cities. Many people want to slip in and out of worship without being noticed.

Churches that make a big deal of having visitors stand and introduce themselves think they are really impressing their visitors. On the contrary, that act likely embarrasses people more than it impresses them. Having visitors introduce themselves also flies in the face of surveys that show Americans have great fear of public speaking. Even introducing themselves in a worship service is very unnerving for many. However, visitors want to experience personal warmth in a church, and they will be impressed by people coming up to them with a special greeting.

Receiving a Visitor Friendly Offering

The unfounded notion that the church is primarily greedy for money used to be one of the biggest turnoffs for the unchurched. That may still be true. Therefore, when they do visit a church, they notice how the offering is taken. Some churches really impress their visitors by not even taking an offering. You have to find the offering box in the narthex if you want to make a contribution.

While most churches do take an offering, it can be done with grace. Visitors can be put at ease at the offering time, if the liturgist says words to this effect, "The ushers will now come forward to receive our offering. If you are a guest today, please sit back and relax as the members of our church give their tithes and offerings to the work of Jesus Christ." It gives permission to the visitor to not give anything. I used this wording, and one visitor said after a service, "Wow, the way you receive the offering is wonderful. As a visitor it had the reverse effect on me. I felt like putting a large bill in the plate!"

Getting Feedback from Visitors

Churches interested in knowing how visitors reacted to their services can add a feedback card to their follow-up letter. Visitors will more likely respond to a simple card with blanks to check or multiple-choice questions. A card asking for feedback might look like this:

> Please help us in our ministry by completing and returning this stamped, self-addressed card.
>
> 1. Felt welcomed: great _____ average_____ poor_____
> 2. Worship music: great _____ average_____ poor_____
> 3. Sermon: great _____ average _____ poor_____
> 4. Nursery: great _____ average _____ poor_____
> 5. Sunday school: great _____ average _____ poor_____
> 6. Building atmosphere: great_____ average _____ poor_____
> 7. God was honored: great _____ average _____ poor_____
> 8. Overall response: great _____ average _____ poor_____
>
> Our first desire is to help people worship Jesus Christ. Kindly offer any suggestions you have to help us fulfill that mission.

Congregations that are truly interested in reaching the unchurched may receive insights from visitors that will help them enhance the quality of their worship experience.

God Uses Websites to Welcome Visitors

What about your website? Do you keep it up-to-date? We had some of our finest people join Friendship Church because of our website, and they drove some distance in order to attend. One young couple living in another city found our church through the website. They drove fifteen to twenty minutes to come to worship; they joined the church and then became very involved. Finally, they bought a house in our community to be closer to their church. That's the power of a good website.

Asking the Excellence Question

If one looks at the creation of God, one realizes that everything was made with amazing excellence. When one ponders the life of Jesus Christ, one sees true greatness. Experiencing the Holy Spirit is a gift of great wonder. We only honor God when we adopt a passion for excellence in everything regarding the church.

At my last church we adopted a vision statement that said, "Friendship Church does everything with excellence unto God." We often asked ourselves about our work, *Is this excellent? Does the quality of what we are doing honor God? Is our work done so well that God is honored by it?* Constantly asking these questions will give the Holy Spirit opportunity to lift the quality of life in the church in general, as well as in welcoming people to a church.

Discussion questions

1. Share your first impression of our church.
2. How can we make our church more welcoming? Evaluate everything that happens, and consider each aspect of it.
3. Are our greeters and ushers trained to both warmly welcome and inform visitors?
4. How can we improve the signs in our building?
5. Is there something in our building that could be made more welcoming? Is there anything that would be a negative distraction to a visitor?
6. What can we offer with more excellence unto God?
7. If we organize parking lot ushers, who will do it and when?

12

Small Groups: Why Have Small Groups in a Small Church?

Great Commission churches work very hard at reaching people for Jesus Christ and then concern themselves with how to help the people grow in their faith. These churches know that growing godly people is their only mission, and when they do that their churches are healthy and usually grow.

All growing churches put lifting the relationship of the congregation to Jesus Christ as their first concern. There is nothing more important. The spiritual climate of the church determines the quality of everything that happens in the life of that congregation.

Healthy congregations have strong small group programs, because they know God uses small groups to help Christians grow and to help build the kingdom of God. They are known as a church *of* small groups rather than a church *with* small groups.

Deepest Spiritual Growth Comes Best in Small Groups

God uses small groups in a special way. Jesus said, "Where two or three are gathered in my name, I am there among them" (Matt 18:20). He was affirming the power of small groups. Small congregations need small groups as much as larger congregations need them. God enriches the lives of the disciples of Jesus Christ in unique ways in small groups.

Personal devotions, including daily prayer and Bible reading, are vitally important for developing a closer relationship with God. Public worship is essential to remaining alive as a disciple of Jesus Christ. However, as crucial as private devotions and public worship are for remaining faithful to Jesus Christ, participating in a small group provides growth not possible in private devotions or public worship.

Personal prayer allows the most intimate relationship with God. Private prayer enables the human heart to get wonderfully close to the heart of God. As important as this is, the Christian spirit needs more in order to be complete. It needs interaction with others, and this interaction gives God the opportunity to provide growth in special ways. This interchange with others in a small group setting allows the Holy Spirit to refine thought and hone the human spirit in a unique manner.

Public worship allows the disciple to praise and honor God within a congregation. Singing hymns with others glorifying God's greatness, hearing God's word read and expounded upon while listening with others, sharing in public prayers, and joining in corporate fellowship are necessary experiences for the Christian disciple. However, public worship does not allow the dialogue, the sharing of ideas and thoughts, which small groups provide. Growth comes by being able to share in conversation with others in a small group setting.

Healthy Churches Are Transformational Churches

Growing churches are also transformational churches. Lives are being changed, which motivates people to be part of such churches. They see that God is making a difference in their lives, and this feels good and right. When individual lives are transformed, when marriages are renewed and deepened, and when families are made healthier and happier through a church, God is going to develop growth in that congregation.

These kinds of transformations take place in small groups. Faith is deepened through Bible studies, as the scriptures are discussed. Marriages are enriched as couples develop a deepening faith together and learn together in small group discussions dealing with marriage issues. Parenting is made easier and more effective as parents talk about their experiences in small groups, and when they learn new parenting skills along with other parents.

All of this happens most effectively in small groups, where people can share their personal experiences. Small groups allow give and take where people share information and life happenings. Growth happens when people can open up and share. Life changes beautifully through dialogue in small groups.

Relationships Are Deepened in Small Groups

Jesus is able to build churches when personal bonds are developed between members and friends of the church. Without these loving relationships growth cannot take place. Knowing seven people is considered by some church authorities as an indicator as to whether a person is really integrated into a congregation.

Small groups aid in assimilating people into a church. After having visited a congregation a few times, newcomers must become involved in a small group in order to give the Holy Spirit the greatest opportunity to help them build bonds with others. There they learn that they have many things in common with persons in the group. Perhaps they know some of the same people, or discover that they have lived in the same communities, have had similar jobs, or share other common experiences.

Member of a Small Group or Member of the Church?

Membership in a small group and membership in the church are not mutually exclusive. However, first involving new people in a small group can be far more meaningful than persuading them to formally join the church. The small group will create bonding relationships within the congregation, which ultimately will more likely result in more meaningful membership in the church.

As a pastor, because membership seemed so important, I usually worked harder on recruiting new members than on making disciples through small group involvement. I regret that, because my focus on membership, in all honesty, was not that helpful to the people or to the congregation. Strong membership growth looked good on the statistical chart at the end of each year, but often that growth did not show up on the worship attendance chart. Having the names of people on the membership books is far less valuable than incorporating people into small groups, where their faith in Jesus Christ can be nurtured. Ideally, membership would follow participation in a small group.

When Membership Is a Rope of Sand

John Wesley can be our model for building the church around small groups. He was the genius who started it all. When Wesley preached he also organized small groups made up of those whose lives were changed. That is why the various Methodist bodies exist around the world; without those small groups, this segment of Christianity would be nonexistent today. George Whitefield was a more dynamic preacher then John Wesley, but Whitefield did not organize his converts into small classes. Later in life, Whitefield reportedly said that Wesley was so wise, because Wesley, with these small groups, had an organization of Christians, but, regretfully, Whitefield had only "a rope of sand."

I have been in the same situation as of George Whitefield. Even though I received many hundreds into membership over the years, they often did not become part of a small group and became a rope of sand. They continued to worship faithfully at first, but their regular worship patterns decreased; sometimes within six months to a year they had completely disappeared from the church scene. They exited through the rear door because their lives were not being changed after coming in the front door.

Churches who focus only on recruiting new members will find that the new members do not become grafted into the tree of the church. They may come to worship sporadically, and the church may be able to involve them in small tasks, but that does not mean they are an integral part of the congregation. Involving the new members in a task or role helps them to feel a part of the church, but that is different from enrolling them in a small group.

Recruiting new members for tasks or roles or even ministry groups is good, as we grow through serving. However, new members often are not strong enough spiritually to jump right into service without first growing in Jesus Christ. Without the inner power and warmth of the Holy Spirit filling their lives, new church members can burn out in a hurry. Small groups meeting weekly, biweekly, or even monthly provide growth experiences that empower new and older disciples for service.

Iron Sharpens Iron in Small Groups

The book of Proverbs says, "Iron sharpens iron, and one person sharpens the wits of another" (27:17). People are needed in our lives to help us grow. We are so self-centered that we tend to protect ourselves from painful change, but change is necessary in order for growth to take place. Without group support, we may be reluctant to change, not see the need for change, or lack the creativity to see new possibilities for helpful change.

I have seen the rough edges of people honed through small group experiences. Some people may have come into a group rather controlling and loud. However, through learning to listen to others in the group, these persons change as the Holy Spirit shows them that others also have value and need to be cared for. They come to realize that their issues are not the only ones in the world and that it can be deeply satisfying to listen to the concerns of others.

When iron sharpens iron the friction produces heat, and sometimes conversations can get hot in a small group, as people grow together. People challenge each other, sharing their different opinions and experiences. A skillful leader can guide tense conversations into wonderful growing experiences. When the small group meets in a prayerful manner and is led by wise leaders, the intense times end up with joyous growth. Most often in the countless small groups I have led, the sweetness of the Holy Spirit has prevailed to bring meaningful change. Growth was never painless, but the new birth of learning was deeply peaceful.

People wishing to grow can use a small group to help hold them accountable. Finding loving, wise people to help them become what they wish to become is not easy, but a wonderful, small group can help make that possible.

How Does a Small Church Offer Small Groups?

A small group begins with the leadership of the church being committed to making disciples of Jesus Christ. That commitment then needs to be undergirded with prayer. The small group experience is so important for the church that it is worth inviting the whole congregation to support this effort in prayer.

On the practical level there are three components to offering small groups: leaders, participants, and curriculum. Discovering and recruiting knowledgeable people with leadership skills is challenging. Perhaps the most effective way to get small group leaders is to train them through a small group experience. A skilled pastor or layperson can begin a small group with the purpose of using it not only for the growth of the group but also for the purpose of training leaders of small groups. Healthy small groups have apprentice leaders in training to begin their own small groups.

Participants enter small groups in various ways. When exciting study material is advertised in worship services and the church newsletter, people get hooked on wanting to learn about that subject. Response cards in the bulletin allow people to sign up during worship, placing the card in the offering plate. Obviously, small group leaders can effectively recruit members through personal contacts as well.

Offering study groups on a semester basis works well. Faithbridge United Methodist Church in Houston, Texas, was just five years old and had 1,000 worshiping on weekends. Why? It was because they had 125 small groups. Most of them were semester-based studies, running from August to December and January to June. Faithbridge was a small membership church at one point, but God used small groups to help it grow large.

An amazing amount of study material is available for small groups today. It is available in Christian bookstores, in magazines, and on the Internet. Study resources are available on virtually any subject or issue of the day. Video studies can be purchased that make leading a group rather simple. Many denominations have video libraries, where churches can get material free of charge.

One small group model used across America involves video teaching. In this model, people are asked in worship if they would "HOST" a small group in their homes for six weeks. This involves four things: H for a heart for God, O to open their home for a group meeting, S for serving coffee, and T to turn on the VCR. The task of the discussion leader is passed around to a different person each week. Phenomenal stories have resulted from this model.

A Story of a Changed Life through a Small Group

Before all of the current material on small groups was available, I ran two men's groups and one women's group using a very simple agenda. We used no literature except referring to the Bible occasionally. Our agenda was for each participant to answer five questions: (1) How am I relating to myself? (2) How am I relating to God, Jesus Christ, and the Holy Spirit? (3) How am I relating to my significant others? (4) How am I relating to my work? (5) How am I relating to friends, neighbors, and strangers?

The weekly meetings lasted about an hour, and each person was given an opportunity to respond to each of these questions. Since each group had about six people, each participant was given about 10 minutes to share. Each session ended in a prayer circle. Many lives were touched through these groups, faith was sustained, relationships were refined, and families were strengthened.

There were many life-changing experiences in those groups. One such experience was that of Tom. He was a big, burly fellow over six feet tall and weighing about two hundred fifty pounds. Tom was married and had a nine-year-old third grader, Matt. Tom had been raised by a strict disciplinarian father, who had a career in the military.

When we began our group in late September, Tom was frustrated because Matt was getting Ds on his schoolwork, and his name was written on the chalkboard almost daily for bad behavior. Tom had been using the same harsh discipline with Matt that he had learned from his father, but gradually, through the love of the group, Tom changed his behavior toward his son. Instead of being harsh with him, Tom began giving Matt a daily, loving bear hug. This loving act had a deep impact on Matt. His grades went up, and his name no longer appeared on the chalkboard.

Tom was a supervisor in a large factory. He told our small group that during his twenty-minute commute to work, he now prayed the Jesus Prayer, "Lord Jesus Christ, have mercy on me." While walking from his car in the parking lot to the plant, he sang a little chorus from our worship service. Tom reported that as he got closer to Jesus Christ through our group, he changed his language and dropped profanity from his vocabulary. Then he shared that his behavior had changed the behavior of the people he was supervising. When he stopped swearing, so did they.

It was evident in Tom's wife's face that she also appeared to have been touched with the growing love in her husband's life. When they were transferred to another state, Tom said to me, "No realtor is going to show me a house on Sunday morning; the first thing we will do when we move to our new community is to find a church." During the nine months that Tom participated in the small group, the Holy Spirit had profoundly moved on this man's life, changing him, his family, and his work environment. Why? Because of the power of Jesus Christ, manifested through a small group.

Discussion questions

1. How can we make our church a church of small groups?
2. What plan can we create that will enable us to do that?
3. Because it's easier for people to join new groups rather than existing ones, what new small groups can we start right away?
4. How can we get most of our people involved?
5. Where will we get leadership to build this culture of small groups in our church?
6. Will we ask group leaders to apprentice other group leaders, so that we will constantly have new groups forming?

13

Leadership Skills: Excelling as an Effective Leader

Small membership churches share similar leadership issues with large membership churches. Everything starts at the top, whether it is a family, a church, a baseball team, a business, or a governmental agency. Leadership is indeed everything. The person at the top of an organization has enormous impact on that group. When an organization is going gangbusters, it is because of capable leadership. Conversely, when an organization flounders, it is almost always because of a leadership problem.

A pastor can view leadership's tremendous impact on a church either as a scary responsibility or as a gift. Energetic, creative pastors, filled with hope, see the power of leadership with positive eyes. They see the possibilities that this influence allows. Thus, the pastor has the wonderful ability to sway a congregation into positive change.

Pastoral authority may be compromised in some small membership churches where the laity have had to run the church themselves, because of lack of pastoral leadership or frequent pastoral change. It may also be compromised in a church that is funded by only a few families who shoulder much of the work in order to keep it running. In those churches, the pastor will have to learn to fit into the power structure before being able to assert major influence.

Leadership Is a Great Privilege

Being blessed to give pastoral leadership to a local church is a great gift and an honor. When God entrusts a pastor to serve a congregation, that is a privilege. It provides the opportunity for the pastor to be used by Jesus Christ in order to teach about God's great truths, to influence lives for holy living, to bring people to a saving faith in Jesus Christ, to help families move toward wholeness, and to help people become more than they could be without the Holy Spirit in their lives. A loving, effective pastor of a local church touches individuals, families, the community, and often a region for Jesus Christ.

The spirit and attitude of a pastor will determine the effectiveness of his or her leadership. People are quick to detect the mind and spirit of their pastor. Humility is readily seen and appreciated. Unfortunately, a spirit of pride and a sense of power are also quickly detected, making people watchful. The pastor who considers it a privilege to serve a church will gain honor, while the pastor who thinks the congregation is the privileged one will reap disdain.

Ironically, Servant Leadership Creates the Biggest Bang

As contradictory as it sounds, servant leaders make the biggest impact. The self-important, macho pastor repels more than impresses. After three years of living with Jesus and observing him, it is amazing that the disciples were arguing the night before his death about who was the greatest among them. They still didn't get it. Jesus, perhaps a little frustrated, took it as a teaching moment. He said, "The greatest among you must become like the youngest, and the leader like one who serves" (Luke 22:26). He told them that they would become great through their service.

Leaders of the church are to practice servant leadership. Our example is Jesus, "who, though he was in the form of God, did not regard equality with God as something to be exploited, but emptied himself, taking the form of a slave, being born in human likeness. And being found in human form, he humbled himself and become obedient to the point of death—even death on a cross" (Phil 2:6-8).

110

We are called to lead churches for the sake of Jesus Christ and the people of God. Therefore, the effective leaders humble themselves before God and empty themselves for the purpose of bringing people to God.

Effective Servant Leaders Have a Mission

As a pastor, being a servant leader means laying down your life for your people; as Jesus said, "I am the good shepherd. The good shepherd lays down his life for the sheep" (John 10:11). Servant leadership means loving your people by visiting them, counseling them, marrying them, baptizing them, and burying them. I hope you feel, as I have always felt, so privileged to be a pastor, because people open up to you in the most trusting ways. They invite you into their lives with amazing openness. In that privileged relationship, God provides opportunity for the pastor to love; sometimes love is shown through comforting and at other times through teaching. God calls pastors to love people.

Loving God and loving people means not only caring for the congregation but also reaching beyond the walls of the church. A servant leader leads, and that means leading the church in the community and in the world. Effective pastors know that the purpose of the church is to make disciples of Jesus, and the prospective disciples are found in the community.

This mission ought to be the passion of every pastor, and thus, it should determine how you spend your time and energy. This means having a passion for helping people find new life in Jesus Christ that will bring about transformation. Yes, the pastoral work is important; but it has to involve more than maintenance. Effective pastors know the difference between changing people's lives and simply taking care of them. Helping to shape loving hearts includes pastoral care, but it is more than holding hands in nursing homes. Although Wesley had great interest in the physical health of the people in his day, he believed that the first business of the church is to save souls.

Servant Leadership Is All about Love

Ministry, like the Christian life, is all about love. The pastor makes loving God with heart, mind, and soul the first priority in life. Nothing is more important than loving and serving Jesus Christ. Being open to the sweet movement of the Holy Spirit is the first concern of the servant leader.

Jesus said that after giving our deepest love to God, we are to love our neighbors as ourselves. Loving neighbor presupposes loving ourselves. The second thing the servant pastor does is to take care of herself or himself. We can serve God and people most effectively only if *we* are happy, healthy and whole. This includes giving loving attention to our families, as well as eating properly, and exercising.

Then the servant leader goes about the business of loving people. That's what pastoral leadership is all about. It's loving people in many ways in order to bring them to Jesus Christ. Shortly after retiring I was invited by my annual conference to fill a pulpit in a Chicago area church for three months. When I met with the interviewing committee for the church, a woman asked me, "What is your plan?" I said, "My plan is to love you." The people and I, indeed, developed a wonderful love relationship during that three-month period. God did some good work in the lives of the people, and in the church, and Jesus Christ was glorified.

Are You Locked in a Box?

If you feel inadequate in your leadership skills, don't lose heart. Leadership is learned. None of us is born a leader, but rather, we learn how to become leaders.

There are a number of things you can do to let God help you become an outstanding leader. Learning from others has helped all of us in one way or another. We all have stood on the shoulders of others. Look around and find effective pastors, and try to learn from them. Don't be hesitant or ashamed to call a few pastors who are wonderfully successful and ask if you can spend time with them. Take them out to lunch and pick their brains about how they run their churches. Ask if you can see their budgets. Find out how they put together all the programs they have going.

Adam Hamilton is the pastor of the United Methodist Church of the Resurrection in Leawood, Kansas. At the age of twenty-seven, he was appointed to a small church of about twenty. Twelve years later, at the age of thirty-nine, God had helped him build the church to 11,500 members. It is the largest church of any denomination in Kansas City. One of the things Adam did was to take a six-month sabbatical, during which time he visited twenty-six of the largest churches in America. Every weekend he was at a different congregation. God used his willingness to learn from others to enable him to do great work in his church.

I had lunch with the pastor of Crossroads Church in Naperville, Illinois. It has fifteen hundred people coming to worship. He told me that Willow Creek Church in Barrington, Illinois, assigned an elder to meet with him weekly for two years. The pastor had the privilege of having a sounding board and someone who could give him new ideas. The pastor gave the impression that these meetings were very helpful to him in his work.

Perhaps you can find a mentor. Clergy at every age can benefit from having someone with whom they can share their work. It takes courage and humility to seek out a mentor, for a variety of reasons. Clergy who are open to seeking the help of a mentor want to be cautious, because they want the right fit. The effectiveness and value of the mentoring relationship will depend upon the comfort of the one being mentored. Unless it feels good not much will come of it.

There are many leadership books available today. You can get books on virtually every aspect of leadership there is. I used to read the business section of the *Chicago Tribune* because of the parallels of leadership in the church and in business. Before electronic media came along, I remember counting about fifteen different papers, magazines, and journals that I received and read regularly. If your personal budget is tight, ask the church to subscribe to some of these for you. The Internet is an incredible gift, and there are also seminars available. Keep learning all you can.

Giving Great Leadership Despite Weaknesses

You may not feel very confident about your leadership skills. Remembering how wonderfully God used leaders with various weaknesses during biblical times can bolster your confidence. Leith Anderson writes that it is a myth that leaders must have all the right traits. Then he gives these examples:

Articulate:	Moses had a speech impediment.
Desire to lead:	Moses preferred to decline. Jonah ran away.
Moral:	David was an adulterer and a murderer.
Wise:	Solomon corrupted Israel with foreign wives and gods.
Relational:	Paul couldn't get along with Barnabas (and others).
Visionary:	Christopher Columbus didn't know where he was going and didn't know where he was when he got there.
Tolerant:	Martin Luther was intolerant of peasants (and others).
Able to invite loyalty:	Abraham Lincoln carried a minority of the popular vote[1]

Pastoral ministry is very complex, and few clergy are effective in *every* aspect of the work. Some are best at pastoral work. Others excel in preaching. Still others feel most competent at administrative work. Some writers urge clergy to do what they are good at doing. That is good advice, but then you have to recruit people to do what you can't do or to help you where you are weak. Some pastors are wonderful pastors and preachers but lousy administrators. So they wisely surround themselves with paid personnel or volunteers who are excellent in administration.

What are your strengths and your weaknesses? Sharpen your strengths, and develop your weaknesses. Become better where you are good, and become good where you are weak. No matter what leadership gifts you think you lack, God is able to do great work in and through you. Believe in your call, then work and pray.

Character Matters

Character is a huge piece in the puzzle of effective leadership. Walking closely with God is not just a devotional exercise. It develops character, which is as important to pastoral ministry as oxygen is to the body. Without oxygen the body obviously ceases to exist, and without character there will be no effective pastoral ministry.

Paul wrote to the Christians in Galatia, "The fruit of the Spirit is love, joy, peace, patience, kindness, generosity, faithfulness, gentleness, and self-control" (Gal 5:22-23). Such fruit will be evident in pastors who are open to the Holy Spirit in their daily lives.

In contrast, Paul also wrote, "Now the works of the flesh are obvious: fornication, impurity, licentiousness, idolatry, sorcery, enmities, strife, jealousy, anger, quarrels, dissensions, factions, envy, drunkenness, carousing, and things like these" (Gal 5:19-21).

Jesus said that our guidelines for all human behavior are wrapped up into two laws—loving God and loving others as we love ourselves. Loving God with all that we are will fill us with the Holy Spirit, so that the fruit of the Spirit is seen through us. Living closely with Jesus Christ gives us wisdom and grace to love people with all that we are. A disciplined prayer life allows God to shape our character and transform our leadership.

The reputation of the professional Christian ministry has fallen on hard times. Protestant clergy and Roman Catholic priests are frequently in the news because of moral allegations. Polls show that Americans do not regard clergy with the respect that they were given thirty years ago. However, the godly character of a clergyperson still influences laity more than the polls.

Success Needs More Than Faithfulness

For decades some clergy have said that it is more important to be faithful than to be successful. Success was usually linked to numerical growth in worship attendance or membership. One still hears this language, and obviously faithfulness must undergird the ministry of every pastor. But, what does faithfulness mean?

Is faithfulness being at the church office from nine o'clock AM until five o'clock PM, preparing a sermon, leading weekly worship, visiting the sick, managing the programs of the church, and maintaining a happy atmosphere in the congregation? There used to be a time when churches were satisfied with pastors who put in their hours, were kind to the congregation, and fulfilled the basic roles of pastor. Whether there was excellence in everything happening in the life of the church, whether the church was really a healthy church, or whether the membership and worship numbers were stagnant didn't really concern the people. People saw their pastor was faithful, and they rewarded him or her for it.

Today, effective pastors realize that faithfulness alone is not adequate in creating excellence. Effective pastors care about being faithful, but they want to be more. They make themselves available to God in order to bring loving transformation to their churches. Effective pastors don't just put in their time; they prioritize it and spend it wisely. Pastors concerned about creating excellence in the small membership church read widely and constantly study new possibilities for their work. They seek God's will for their churches.

Effective pastors do not think about what will appease a congregation. They do not ask themselves, "What can I get by with?" That kind of minimal thinking seldom enters their minds. Instead of asking, "What does this congregation want?" They ask, "What does God want for this congregation?"

In my life I have found a parallel between pastoral work and marriage. When I sought first the will of God, my congregations were happy. The same has been true in marriage. When I related most closely with Jesus Christ, then my marriage was the strongest. Loving God above all else gave me grace to love my wife and to love my church most deeply.

My guess is that most members of small membership churches are very tolerant of their pastoral leadership. In many cases they are just happy to have a pastor. Most will be impressed if their pastor is "faithful" in the work.

However, healthy and growing small membership churches presuppose faithfulness, but expect effectiveness. Just being on the job is no longer adequate. The question is, "Are you getting the job done?" This may be particularly true of suburban churches that are full of business and professional people. They expect the same quality leadership in the church that they experience in business. These parishioners are often bottom-line people. They expect the effectiveness of their pastor to be demonstrated through excellent leadership. They want programs that meet their needs, and they feel best when associated with an effective pastor. Putting in time is not adequate for them. They want to see results. If they do not see them, they will find a congregation that gives them what they want.

Keeping Up with the Treadmill

Life is a gigantic treadmill, and there is no getting off. It has no buttons to push, allowing us to speed up or to slow down the pace. We either keep up with the movement of the belt of life, or we fall down. The world is changing so rapidly, that unless we keep on learning we are not going to be effective pastors.

A seminary degree involving three years of study is only the beginning of a pastor's learning process. God can do the most effective work through pastors who are constantly reading, studying, and learning. New things are happening in worship with technology, with music, and with organizational thinking. In order to talk intelligently with your laity and preach sermons that are relevant, you have to read widely. Effective pastors must be lifelong learners.

In seminary pastors are seldom trained adequately for administrative and supervisory work. Seminaries are called theological schools because they focus on theology. Practical courses are also taught, but much of the work of pastoral ministry has to be learned on the job, in the local church, or through additional focused seminars.

When I entered the full-time pastoral ministry, I was very enthusiastic about theology, but I was totally unprepared for the practical aspects of ministry. I came into the local church out of sync with the laity. Oh, I related well with the people, but they were not so focused on theology as I was. Knowing the three views of atonement, and knowing the difference between pre-, post-, and a-millennialism is very interesting. However, I think that helping people with godly living from Monday through Friday and training them as disciples of Jesus Christ is far more significant. I was far better equipped to talk theology than I was to bring people to Christ, to help them grow, and to help them put their faith into daily practice.

Discussion questions

1. What do I think are some of my leadership strengths?
2. What are some areas where I need work, and how can I work at improving those areas?
3. What issues are keeping me from being the most effective leader I can be?
4. What resources should I explore to help me grow?
5. Where can I find people who could be role models for me?
6. Is there a wise, capable person in my life who would be willing to mentor me? If so, am I open to it and willing to pursue it? If so, when and how will this take place?

Note

1. Leith Anderson, *Leadership That Works* (Minneapolis: Bethany House, 1999), 41.

14

Growth Challenges: Positive Change with Minimum Negativity

S mall membership churches control their future. They are in charge of what will happen to them. Yes, social factors have a huge impact; but within the arena of sociological change, small membership churches still are able to determine their future.

Change Is the Only Constant in Life

The only constant in life is change. Change comes to our bodies, our relationships, our churches, our communities, our country, our world, and even how we relate to God. All churches are constantly going through change. Increased mobility in society and the practice of church-jumping have heightened the movement of parishioners in and out of churches. Membership changes take place constantly, particularly in suburban churches. Aging mainline churches constantly experience huge change through the death of their members. Change through death and people leaving a community are beyond the church's control; however, every church has power to control positive change.

Grabbing the Bull of Change by the Horns

Most people don't realize that change in a church is inevitable yet manageable. Many people in churches where membership has reached a plateau do not understand that silent change is still taking place, although they have not noticed it. It is helpful to enlighten folks and help them realize that the most favorable way to deal with change is to be in charge of it.

Many churches are frustrated and reach a plateau because they have allowed change to control them, instead of their controlling it. These words have been repeated many times in recent years, "If you always do what you have always done, you will always get the same results." Churches get into ruts and become comfortable. Since it is risky to pull out of a rut when driving a car, people fear what might happen if their church tries to go in new directions.

Most churches are not at the mercy of uncontrolled change. They have power to control much of their destiny. Small membership churches should not feel helpless when things start to change. Although change is inevitable, good change can be created. Alive and healthy churches are always creating change. That is part of growing and following the guidance of the Holy Spirit. Change is inevitable if we are reaching people for Jesus Christ. Effective churches realize that they have no choice but to make changes. However, they do not change for change's sake but for God's sake. They are not interested in figuratively rearranging the furniture of the church, but they wish to follow the lead of the Holy Spirit in reaching people for Jesus Christ.

Creating change can be very positive. When clergy and laity see new possibilities for improving the life of a church and work together to bring these improvements into being, it creates joy and excitement. Adding new small groups where people are thrilled with new learning energizes a whole church. Having new members and young people step into major leadership roles refreshes programs. Creating new mission and outreach programs infuses goodwill into a congregation.

Most relational problems are caused by unmet expectations. Therefore, conflict is reduced when a pastor and church have good communication. The wise pastor communicates his or her expectations with the leaders of the church. In like manner, the congregation needs to share its expectations with the pastor as well.

Dealing with Foot Draggers

Creating change can also bring negative reaction. We all tend to enjoy the familiar; therefore, we become comfortable doing things the way we have always done them. Old routines are hard to break. Long established organizational habits become deeply ingrained. Therefore, change is often met with opposition. Even when wonderful changes come to your church, you can hit a brick wall of resistance. The leadership team has to decide if they will allow a small group of dissenters to stop the growth of the church. Will "foot draggers" be allowed to sabotage the strategy of the church? Will they be allowed to stand in the way of life and vitality? Change can cause conflict, but it does not have to create chaos.

Wanting to change the Sunday morning schedule or the content of the worship services often brings negative reaction. Visionary pastors and church leaders often bring criticism because they are alive and want the church to move forward. What you have to worry about is how to keep change from dividing and splitting the church. If you have the well-being of the church at heart, if you want to truly make disciples of Jesus Christ, if you are sensitive and caring in your approach and people still threaten to leave, *let them go*. Naturally, you always feel badly when someone leaves the church, but sometimes you cannot avoid it. I was surprised, particularly during a building program, when some folks left because they said the church was getting too big. They wanted a smaller church.

Efforts to Bring Everyone on Board

Wise and loving church leadership teams learn to manage conflict. In churches that are alive, vital, and growing, conflict comes with the territory. When there is something new happening, or where something requires change, differences of opinion emerge.

How do we minimize conflict? Loving leaders do everything they can to administer their churches in a loving and wise way. The first step is for the leadership to know exactly what change they propose, why they are proposing it, and how it will make the church more effective. Loving leaders do not propose change to be gimmicky or trendy. When we raised twenty thousand dollars for projectors and computers, some said, "Why spend all this money for entertainment?" They didn't have a clue that God uses this wonderful technology to reach people for Jesus Christ, and that this was neither contrived nor an effort at doing something just because it was becoming a popular trend.

It is important that you have a meaningful mission statement that has been adopted by the leadership of your church. If you have such a statement, live by it. Lift it up regularly to your people, and make all of your programming fit within this statement. When you add new programs or make other changes, ask how they fit with your mission statement. Will this new approach help us to fulfill our mission statement more effectively? If you confront criticism about a change, show how the new program fits your mission statement. The mission statement should be your North Star, directing and supporting the changes being made.

The leadership of the church should be involved in change. The wise pastor gains the support of the leadership of the congregation before making changes. The people who pay the bills have a right to choose what is happening in their church. It is important that new programs are not perceived as the pastor's personal agenda. Rather, they need to be seen as a product of the leadership team. Even if you are buying a new two-thousand-dollar lawn mower, the request should come through the people in charge. Let them propose the purchase. The wise pastor does not spring change on his or her people.

Help your people see that God has a will for your church, and enable people to see that being faithful to God's call is more important than our individual desires and preferences. Some may not be pleased to have the eleven o'clock service on Sunday morning completely changed to a contemporary service. However, if they understand that it may attract more young couples to Jesus Christ and the church, they will be more accepting of it.

Good, clear communication minimizes resistance. Explain what you are doing. Ask the question, "Will this new program help us fulfill our mission more effectively?" Instead of trying to have everyone involved in the formulation of the plan, assign it to a team or task force. Let that group refine the plan and then present it to the church council. If a major change is proposed for worship, it should be announced a few weeks in advance through the church's newsletter and bulletin. Once you are convinced that it is in line with the church's vision and mission, then move ahead.

People need to know the reason for the proposed change. They need to know exactly what the nature of the change is. They need to know that you have considered all the alternatives and believe that this is the best course of action. They need to know the implications of the proposed change—the cost, the timing, and how it will affect them. They also need to see the payoff or the reward.

To Grow or Not to Grow?

Obviously, growing churches are changing churches. You can't grow without change. But, declining churches are also changing. Even plateaued churches are changing congregations, although perhaps less noticeably. It is helpful for laity to understand the constant changing dynamic going on in every church.

From personal experience I have found that change from growth is more exciting than change from stagnancy or decline. Churches afraid of growth change should be assured that growth change can be wonderful. If people can have their vision expanded and see the wonder of others finding new life in Jesus Christ, it should bring them joy.

Positive change begins with the vision of the church as it is expressed in the mission statement. Some of the last words that the resurrected Christ told his disciples were that they were to go out and make new disciples. I believe that this should be part of the mission statement of every church. Vast numbers of small membership churches across America whose first priority is to make disciples of Jesus Christ can grow numerically. Those who cannot grow in numbers will still become healthier churches.

Twelve Commandments about Change

Carver McGriff has an excellent chapter on change in *The Passion Driven Congregation.*[1] He gives Ten Commandments for local pastors, and I will add two of my own. Following these commandments will help pastors overcome dissension in the church and allow Jesus Christ to maintain a loving, healthy, happy, wholesome spirit in the church.

Number One: "Look at Yourself." The first commandment is for the pastor to see himself or herself from the congregation's perspective. Before you initiate change in the congregation, consider how long you have been at the church. Then think about the fact that some congregants have been giving themselves to God in that church, literally, for decades. Many have sacrificed financially to help build the church or to refurnish it. In all fairness and consideration, don't treat your people any differently than you would want to be treated if you were in their shoes.

Number Two: "Don't Solve the Problem from the Pulpit." Don't air church problems from the pulpit that are best dealt with in open meetings. Laity have a right to be able to respond to controversial subjects. It is unfair and unloving to take advantage of the pulpit when nobody can talk back. I have a friend in California whose pastor took church problems into pulpit prayers. Instead of praying to God, he used the prayer time in effect to scold the people. Naturally, it is wonderful to celebrate and talk from the pulpit about church projects that the vast majority favors. Good news about the church from the pulpit is very proper. However, people listen very selectively when controversial subjects are discussed from the pulpit. Church problems ought to be discussed in board meetings, where careful discussion can be held.

Number Three: "Take the Other People Into Your Confidence." Sincerely seek the suggestions of the people who are resistant to change. Instead of ignoring them or bulldozing over them, spend time with them. Honor their viewpoints, explain the changes you are considering, and help them see the benefits to them and to their church. Often churches will have one or two gatekeepers whose views will either help promote ideas or they will keep them from being adopted. Care for these people. I remember one of the men in my first congregation who was opposed to a program I proposed. I spent significant time with him on the issue, and he wrote out one of the biggest checks supporting it.

Number Four: "Don't take sides." Try to stay neutral in your outlook. Remember, you are the pastor of the whole congregation. When changes occur in a church, dissension often occurs. People take differing positions, and it is a temptation for the pastor to side with one group in the church favoring one position. The wise pastor is slow to identify strongly with a position. Try to keep your focus on what will benefit the whole congregation. If some old antagonist is being attacked, avoid jumping in to hurt him or her. The wise pastor works to build a consensus. Get most people thinking together for the common good instead of siding with a small group against everybody else.

There are times when you have to take a position, because you think it is the right one for the church. One year our music director thought we should drop one of our four Christmas Eve services. In a board meeting

I felt it was my job to point out that we would reduce the options for our people by dropping a service, which would probably cut down on the number of people attending by approximately one hundred.

Number Five: "Listen to the people involved." Genuinely hear all the people's viewpoints. Pay attention to their reasoning and also to their heartfelt concerns. Listening to people is one of the most important roles of the pastor. We need to listen with full attention and with understanding. The feelings of people are very important, and we will avoid much pain if we hear what our people are saying.

Number Six: "Put yourself in the other person's place." If we really care for people, we care for their feelings and their thoughts. McGriff says one of the hardest yet most meaningful sentences to say to another person is, "If I were in your place, I would feel exactly as you do." [2] Those are disarming words. When said sincerely and when people hear them, it makes them relax, because they feel understood. Often people will become your allies when they sense that you understand their position.

Number Seven: "Explain the benefits to everyone." Make sure everyone understands the advantages for the congregation and the community. If programs benefit the whole church, or even a segment of the church, help people understand that. People may resist adding a new worship service because they do not realize the benefits it may offer. When we added a Saturday evening service we explained that it would benefit people who were not able to worship on Sundays because of work, and that it would give families a worship opportunity who needed to be away on particular Sundays. Plus, it gave us an opportunity to provide a more informal service for those who preferred such an experience. Reasonable people understand the benefits of change and usually will support change that offers advantages to the church.

Number Eight: "Smile." It truly is amazing what a bright smile, reflecting a happy spirit, can do to a disgruntled soul. A smile is warm water on an ice cube of frustration. We are told it takes fewer muscles to smile than to frown, but the power of those muscles is strong. In the midst of our busy-ness, it is important to remember not to take ourselves too seriously. Singing the chorus about the sweetness of the Holy Spirit is not just a song. Allowing that sweetness to be seen on our faces through our smiles is very important to the spirit of a church.

Number Nine: "Don't argue." McGriff quotes Dale Carnegie, famous for his classes on human relationships, who said, "I have listened to, engaged in, and watched the effect of thousands of arguments. As a result of all this, I have come to the conclusion that there is only one way under high heaven to get the best of an argument—that is to avoid it. Avoid it as you would rattlesnakes and earthquakes."[3] Discussions are one thing, but arguments are another. The wise pastor knows when the line is being crossed. The wise pastor tries to prevent situations where voices are raised and feelings are hot. God usually does not win in those circumstances.

Number Ten: "Be there for them." Our first responsibility as pastors is to care for all the people, even the "crocodiles," in our congregations. We are God's ambassadors for them. They look to us as representatives of Christ. If we push them aside for our own agendas, where can they go?

I add two commandments of my own.

Number Eleven: Practice humility the best you can. Read and reread Philippians chapter 2. It is so hard to lay our egos aside. This is particularly true when your church begins to grow and make significant strides. We think we are causing the growth when it is God.

Number Twelve: Last, develop a praying church. Make prayer a central experience in your own life as well as in your church. Staying in close touch with God is a practical way of acquiring humility and your example will have a peaceful effect on your church.

Discussion questions

1. What are the major changes taking place in our community that affect our church?
2. What are the big changes taking place in our church right now?
3. Are we managing those changes, or are they controlling us?
4. Do we have a conflicting problem in our church right now? If so, how can we lovingly manage it so we can move ahead, serving Jesus Christ most effectively?
5. Do we want to grow? Are we willing to do what it requires to let God bring growth to our church?
6. Are we willing to change so growth can happen in our congregation?

Notes

1. E. Carver McGriff and M. Kent Millard, "Compassionate Change," in *The Passion Driven Congregation* (Nashville: Abingdon, 2003), 109-19.

2. Ibid, 115.

3. Dale Carnegie, *How to Win Friends and Influence People* (New York: Pocket Books, 1936, rev. 1981), 110.